SKILLS IN
GRAPHIC
PRODUCTS

Geoff Hancock

Heinemann

Heinemann Educational Publishers
Halley Court, Jordan Hill, Oxford OX2 8EJ
a division of Reed Educational & Professional Publishing Ltd

OXFORD MELBOURNE AUCKLAND
JOHANNESBURG BLANTYRE GABORONE
IBADAN PORTSMOUTH (NH) USA CHICAGO

Heinemann is a registered trademark of Reed Educational & Professional Publishing Ltd

First published 2000

04 03 02 01 00
9 8 7 6 5 4 3 2 1

British Library Cataloguing in Publication Data
A catalogue record for this book is available from the British Library

ISBN 0 435 42338 X

Designed and typeset by Ken Vail Graphic Design, Cambridge
Cover illustration by Barry Atkinson
Illustrated by Brian Melville, Big Red Hat, Joan Corlass, John Plumb, Linda Rogers & Associates (Peter Dennis).
Printed and Bound in Spain by Edelvives

Acknowledgements

The author would like to thank the pupils of The Kings of Wessex Community School for their help and support in producing this book. Thanks in particular to Judith Brownbill, Mark Fotheringham, Robert Fletcher and Melanie Froud for their Graphic Products work which is included in this book.

The publishers would like to thank the following for permission to produce copyright material and photos:

J. Allan Cash Ltd for the photo on p. 48; Argos for the logo on p. 56; BBC Natural History Unit for the photo on p. 48; Gareth Boden for the photos on pp. 4, 5, 7, 12, 18, 19, 22, 23, 26, 33, 37, 40, 46, 50, 51, 52, 54, 57, 61, 66, 69, 70, 71, 72, 73, 74, 75, 76, 77, 78, 82, 83, 87, 88, 89, 93; Bolton Wanderers Supporters Association for the website images on p. 85; Cadbury for the logo on p. 57 and website images on p. 84; Collections/Chris Honeywell for the photo on p. 67; Collections/Lesley Howling for the photo on p. 67; Empics for the photo on p. 69; Eon Productions/Ronald Grant for the photo on p. 68; Greg Evans for the photos on p. 67, 69; MacDonalds for the logo on p. 56; MIRA for the photo on p. 28; Oxford Scientific Films/Marshall Black for the photo on p. 48; Oxford Scientific Films/Stan Osolinksi for the photo on p. 49; Robert Opie Collection for the photo on p. 69; Photodisc for the photos on p. 79; Rolls Royce for the screendump on p. 81; Shell for the logo on p. 56; SPL/Ed Young for the photo on p. 80; Stone for the photos on pp. 58, 82, 86; Techsoft for the illustration on p. 80 and the photos on p. 83; Virgin for the logo on p. 56.

The publishers have made every effort to trace copyright holders. However, if any material has been incorrectly acknowledged, the publishers would be pleased to correct this at the earliest opportunity.

Tel: 01865 888058 www.heinemann.co.uk

Contents

What are graphic products?	4	Point of sale displays	50
Tools and equipment	6	Nets (developments)	52
The design process	8	Information graphics	54
Getting started on a project	10	Logos and trademarks	56
Doing research	12	Ergonomics	58
Information and presentation	14	What type are you?	60
Charts, graphs and displays	16	Grids and layouts	62
Learning from products	18	Underlays	64
Design ideas	20	The final print	66
Development and final design	22	Posters and merchandizing	68
Planning the make	24	Unwrapping the pack	70
Quality matters	26	Materials for packaging	72
Testing and evaluation	28	Processes	74
Drawing	30	Using ICT	76
Drawing in 3-D	32	Scanners and digital cameras	78
Perspective drawing	34	Computer-aided design	80
Drawing circles and ellipses	36	Computer-aided manufacture	82
Orthographic drawing 1	38	Cyber graphics	84
Orthographic drawing 2	40	Models	86
Light and shade	42	Modelling	88
Using colour	44	Case study in design part 1	90
Effective colour techniques	46	Case study in design part 2	92
Colour in focus	48	**Glossary**	94
		Index	96

What are graphic products?

Graphic products are things that use pictures or words to sell, communicate or protect either themselves or other products. This seems to be an awkward definition so let me give you some examples.

You are currently reading a graphic product. All books communicate information. They use text and graphics in the form of pictures and diagrams. They often have a hard or soft cover to protect the inside pages. They use graphics on the front cover to draw attention to the book and to help sell it.

Graphic products are nearly always made from paper, cardboard or plastic. They can be two-dimensional (2-D) or three-dimensional (3-D). A good example of a 2-D graphic product is a credit card. Made from thin plastic, the credit card communicates information and often has interesting graphics to promote it. A good example of a 3-D graphic product is a cereal box which is made from cardboard and has attractive graphics on the front to grab attention.

Good examples of 2-D and 3-D graphic products

Elements of a graphic product

The main elements of a graphic product are the text, the pictures or images and the style or layout.

The compact disc (CD) is a common household product that shows these three elements well.

The example of the CD shows that, within a graphic product, there is often a range of components or parts. These are all graphic products themselves. In the photo below there is the case which protects the CD, the inlay which communicates information about it, and surface printing on the CD itself which also communicates information about the CD and helps sell it.

A compact disc and its case show the main elements of a graphic product

Text

The text and how it is used can have a large effect upon the graphic product. The text is sometimes bold, is in different styles or typefaces, and is sometimes combined with a graphic to form a **logo**.

For example, the text used on a fire exit sign is very bold and clear. It has a different function from the text used on graphic products such as chocolate wrappers or soft drink cans. Its function is to clearly communicate information.

A fire exit sign

In contrast, the text on a drink's can label (below) is used to help sell the product. This is because it is both part of an attractive design and tells people about the product. It has a different function to the fire exit sign.

A pupil's design for a drink's can label

Pictures or images

The pictures or images used on graphic products are used to communicate information and to sell the product. Pictures or graphic images should always conform to the AIDA test. AIDA stands for:

- Attract
- Interest
- Desire
- Action.

Consider a common graphic product such as food packaging. A mouth-watering picture of the food is nearly always shown. This attracts the potential customer and creates interest in the product. When attracted, the customer takes a closer look at things like the price and the ingredients. If they desire the product they then go on to the final stage which is action – they buy the product.

Packaging should attract interest and create desire

Layout

The layout of a graphic product is how the text and pictures are arranged on it. The design of the layout helps to give the product a certain style.

The way the text and pictures are arranged creates the style of the product

Packaging

Packaging used for products such as perfume or after-shave often has two parts. These are known as primary (first or main) and secondary packaging. The primary packaging in the case of perfume is the bottle or container. The secondary packaging is the outer box. Secondary packaging is often a rectangular cube, so that the irregular shaped container inside can be stacked on the shelf and easily packed in boxes for transportation.

So, graphic products communicate, protect and sell. They are often short-lived (e.g. cinema ticket, advert, poster) and are usually made from inexpensive materials. Millions of pounds are spent each year on graphic products and they are an important part of our lives.

To do

1 a Make a list of as many graphic products as you can think of.

b Carry out the AIDA test on one of the graphic products you have listed.

2 Collect examples of labels, packaging, tickets, flyers, telephone cards, etc. Compare how the main elements (text, pictures and layout) have been used.

Tools and equipment

Designing and producing graphic products requires good skills in the use of tools and equipment. Choosing the right equipment is vital.

Drawing equipment

Pencils

The common pencil is the designer's most important piece of equipment. Pencils can be very hard for producing crisp **feint lines** or soft for sketching and shading.

The grade of the pencil is usually printed on its stem. The grades range from 9H to 9B. The higher the 'H' number, the harder the pencil is. The higher the 'B' number, the softer it is.

 A 2B pencil is soft – it leaves dark lines and is useful for shading or adding tone.

 An HB is medium soft/hard and is a good general purpose pencil.

 A 2H pencil is quite hard and draws crisp feint lines.

Fine line pens

Fine line pens are now popular with designers. They are useful for 'inking' in lines and come in a variety of sizes. The most common sizes are: 0.3mm, 0.5mm and 0.7mm. The size relates to the thickness of the line the pen produces.

Three different fine line pens, showing different line thickness

Rendering

The word **rendering** simply means adding colour to a graphic. By applying colour to a graphic you help bring it to life. There is a wide range of equipment you could use.

Colouring pencils

Colouring pencils are useful for adding different shades of colour. You can produce a darker **tone** simply by pressing harder. The tone is the amount of light and dark used. This is useful for shading.

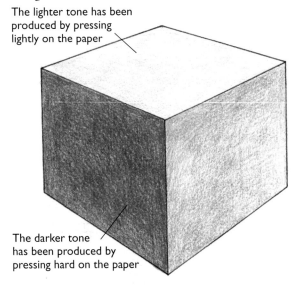

The lighter tone has been produced by pressing lightly on the paper

The darker tone has been produced by pressing hard on the paper

Colouring pencils are also useful for showing **texture**. A texture board can be produced by sticking materials with different textures to a flat board. For example, if you place a texture board with a piece of sandpaper or hardboard on it under the paper you are drawing on, an orange peel effect can be produced.

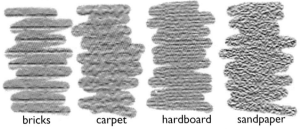

bricks   carpet   hardboard   sandpaper

Different textures produced by using a texture board

Spirit markers

Marker pens are widely used by graphic designers for adding solid or uniform colour. The ink dries quickly and gives a professional finish.

A marker pen has been used to render this drawing

Drawing aids

To help you produce better drawings there are a number of helpful pieces of equipment.

Set squares

Set squares look like triangles. They are used for producing accurate drawings. One type has a 30 degree and a 60 degree angle and is used for **isometric projection**. The other has a 45 degree angle and is used for **oblique projection** and **orthographic projection**.

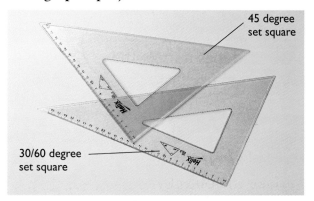

45 degree set square

30/60 degree set square

Compasses and circle templates

Circles can be drawn using a compass. Always use a compass with a screw adjuster for accurate drawing. (Compasses with fine line pen attachments can also be used). Alternatively, a circle **template** can be used to draw circles. Graphic designers use templates for increased speed.

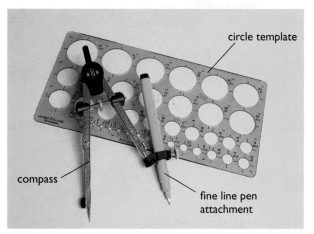

circle template

compass

fine line pen attachment

To do

1 Produce a texture board with as many different surfaces as you can find.

2 Draw a simple cube and use a 2B pencil to shade each face with a different tone.

The design process

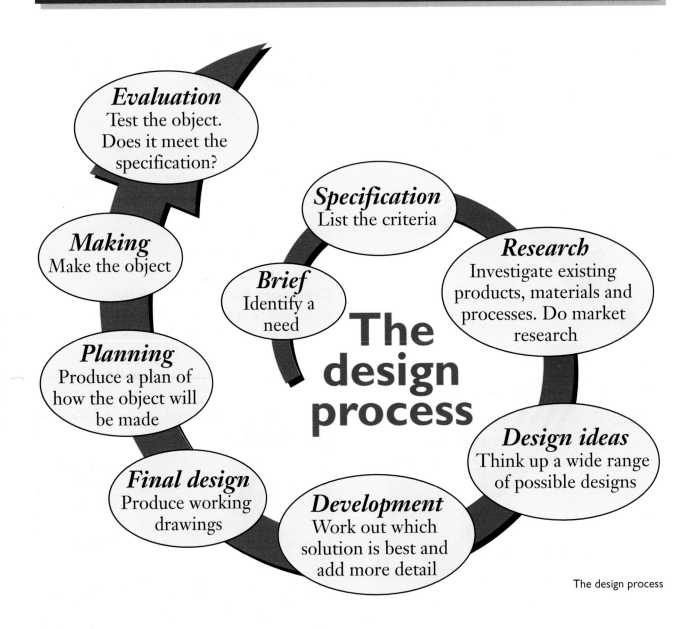

Evaluation
Test the object.
Does it meet the
specification?

Making
Make the object

Planning
Produce a plan of
how the object will
be made

Final design
Produce working
drawings

Brief
Identify a
need

Specification
List the criteria

**The
design
process**

Research
Investigate existing
products, materials and
processes. Do market
research

Design ideas
Think up a wide range
of possible designs

Development
Work out which
solution is best and
add more detail

The design process

The **design process** is the common link that
binds all your technology subjects together.
Designing is about using a range of skills to
solve problems.

For example, you would go through the same
process for the design of a chair or for some food
packaging as you would when designing the new
inlay for a CD.

Brief

Usually graphic designers are given the **brief** by a
client. A brief is a short and clear statement
which says what is needed. Imagine you were
asked to design the cover inlay for a new CD for
a famous band. The brief might say:

'Design and produce a cover for the new CD
Indian Summer'.

Sometimes the graphic designer will have to write the brief themselves. This usually happens when they have their own idea which they will later try and sell to a client.

Analysing the brief

Analysing the brief simply means asking questions about the brief to get some idea about what you can and cannot do.

When you analyse a brief always use the '5WH' approach.

5WH stands for 'Who?, What?, Where?, When?, Why?, How?'. Here are some of the questions you might ask for the CD inlay:

WHO? – who is the **target market**? What age group is the product for? What is their sex? What are their likes and dislikes?

WHAT? – What has the product got to do? What size and shape does it have to be?

WHERE? – Where will the product be sold? Where can I find information about the product?

WHEN? – When must it be finished? When will it be released?

WHY? – Why is it needed? Is an alternative possible? Why must it be that shape and size?

HOW? – How will it be made? How much money will it cost? How many will be made?

The answers to these questions will help you to write a detailed **specification** for the product.

Specification

The specification is one of the most important stages in the design process. It specifies (states in detail) all the things the product must do to be successful. It is usually written as a list. A specification for the CD inlay might look like this:

- It should show a picture of the band
- It should have an image which reflects the title *Indian Summer*
- It should be printed on glossy paper
- It must be a standard size so that it fits all CD cases
- It must be designed in a way that it can be reduced in size to fit a cassette case
- It must be cheap to produce.

The specification is closely linked to the **evaluation**.

Hint

When you write an evaluation go back to each specification point in turn and ask yourself 'Have I met this point?' 'Have I changed it?' 'If so this is my modification.'

To do

1. Write a specification for a poster to promote a school concert. Think about size, cost, pictures/images, information.

2. Using each of the headings for the design process shown on page 8, write out the process for satisfying the problem of your own hunger when arriving home from school.

Getting started on a project

Brainstorming

This is a good way of starting a project. Brainstorming means writing down every idea that comes into your head. It is important not to discount any ideas at this stage.

Brainstorm diagrams are sometimes called spider diagrams – that is because they look like thin legs that come from a central body. Each new idea should be linked by a line to the last idea. This shows how the new idea links to the last. Grouping ideas like this helps when you go onto the next stage and organize your thoughts.

When you have finished your brainstorm think carefully about all the ideas listed. Organize these into helpful and unhelpful suggestions. At this point you should analyse these ideas further. This helps you to identify the most important features of the project.

Hint

Don't just do a brainstorm and then forget about it. It is of no value unless it is used to help you develop an idea for your project.

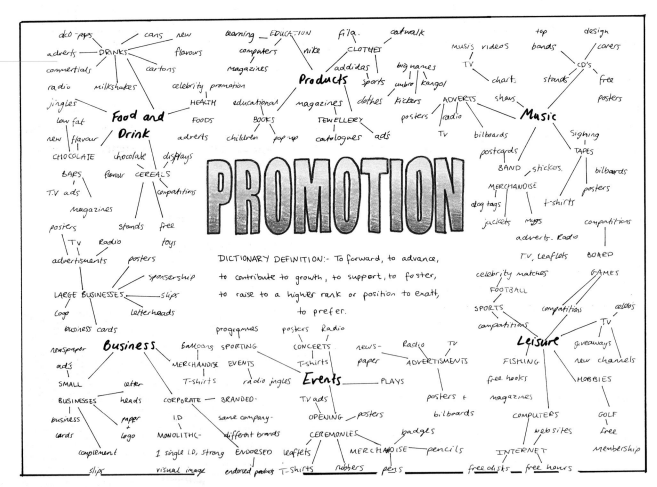

A pupil's promotion brainstorm

	Function	Safety	Reliability	Weight	Efficiency	Storage when not in use	Durability	Strength	Ergonomics & Anthropometrics	Simple Construction	Complex Technologies	Aesthetics	Shape	Form	Colour	Texture	Taste	Smell	Impact	Cost	Value for Money	Cost effective manufacture	Low Cost to Buy	High degree of accuracy needed	High quality of finish required	Environmental	Environmentally safe in use	Recyclable	Ethical and Moral	Not socially damaging	Cultural considerations
Undesirable																															
Not Applicable																															
Unimportant																															
Desirable																															
Important																															
Essential																															
		1	2	3	4	5	6	7	8	9	10		11	12	13	14	15	16	17		18	19	20	21	22		23	24		25	26

Project analysis requires you to look at the whole project in detail and decide which are its most important factors

Project analysis

'How do you eat an elephant?' The answer is in small chunks. Design and technology projects can often appear complicated. Project analysis helps you to break down a project into smaller pieces.

More areas that could be in a graphics product analysis are:

- **Function** – how will it work?
- Materials – what properties are needed?
- Cost – how expensive will it be to produce?
- **Ergonomics** – how will it suit the user?
- How will it be made or printed?

The project analysis diagram helps you to identify the most important aspects of a project. Each aspect of the problem is rated from essential to undesirable. By focusing upon the most important aspects, you are able to find a way through the problem and plan your time efficiently.

Key features

Another way of analysing a project is to make a list of all the key features. It is a good idea to rank these features in order of importance. This will help you to write a specification for the design as the project progresses.

Key features for a business card:

- Size and style of font
- Layout of text
- Use of logo.

To do

1. Do an analysis for new packaging for tennis balls. Ask yourself:
   a How many balls will it hold?
   b Will it need to stack the balls?
   c How will it attract customers?
   d What size will it need to be to hold the tennis balls?

Doing research

Research means the process of finding out information about a design project. Research is not something that is done once during a project and then forgotten about. It should be carried out at many stages throughout a project. Sometimes you need a **questionnaire** to find out what people think about something or you may look at a book or CD-ROM, or use the Internet. Every time you look in a book or ask someone a question, you are doing research.

Sources of information

There are basically two types of research:
1 primary
2 secondary.
Primary research means first-hand information-gathering, such as making a visit or interviewing people. The advantage of primary research is that you investigate the problem in real life rather than having a second-hand view of it.

Secondary research means using information that someone else has produced, for example in a book or magazine. One disadvantage of this is that you often have to work from a picture or image and cannot see what you are researching face to face. Below are some examples of sources for primary and secondary research.

Primary sources
- Visits and interviews
- Analysis of an existing product
- Questionnaires
- Consumer trials (such as offering free trials and then asking for evaluations)

Secondary sources
- Books
- Magazines
- The Internet
- CD-ROMs

Secondary sources of information

Information from computers

Get the most out of your computer

Computers are useful for carrying out research. Websites on the Internet often have pages and pages of information about a product which can help you. It is tempting just to print this out and put it in your project. Before you do, STOP! Ask yourself if the information is relevant. If not, don't use it.

Warning

Pages and pages of printouts from the computer will gain you no marks!

It is only when you do something with the research that it becomes valuable.

Questionnaires

CD Questionnaire

How old are you? ☐

How many CDs do you buy each month? ☐

What attracts you to CD covers? _____

Should there be a picture of the band?
yes ☐ no ☐

A sample questionnaire about CDs

Asking people questions about a product is a good way of gathering information. If you write a questionnaire and carefully record the information, it will help you to make important decisions about such things as the size, colour, shape and cost.

When writing a questionnaire follow these rules:

- Avoid questions that require long answers
- Ask questions that are quick to answer
- Only ask questions that will give you useful information
- Use tick boxes where possible.

The information you collect from the completed questionnaires needs to be sorted and recorded. A simple tally chart is a good way of doing this.

Age 11–12: ⵍⵍⵍ /	Age 12–13: ///
Age 13–14: ⵍⵍⵍ ////	Age 14+: //

A simple tally chart

Alternatively, a computer database can be used for recording the information. This is useful because the database program will quickly produce graphs to show the different responses.

Using a database

A computer database is a piece of software designed to store and retrieve a vast amount of information. You would set up a record for each person who answered the questionnaire. Within each record you would put the questions that were asked. Each different question is called a field.

Once the information has been stored on the database it is easy to use. The database will allow you to sort the information into any order. For example, it will give you a list of answers in alphabetical order or age order. It will also allow you to quickly search for the most popular answer.

The database below would provide a quick answer to the question, 'How many females between the ages of 20–25 are prepared to spend more than £20 on perfume?'

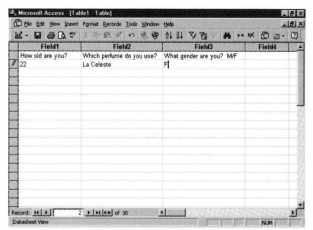

A database screen showing information from a questionnaire

To do

1. Design a questionnaire to find out:
   a people's views on fast food restaurants
   b whether the style of graphics on the packaging used by fast food restaurants influences people.

2. Use a computer database to store this information.

Information and presentation

Results

After you have carried out your research you will have a large amount of information. This information needs to be analysed before you can make an evaluation of your findings. This evaluation will form the results of your research.

The results of your research should always be graphically presented. A picture, graph or chart is much easier to understand and remember than a set of figures.

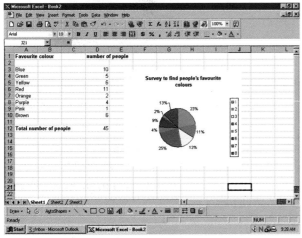

A comparison of written information and a chart

Types of information

There are basically two types of information that come from the results of research:

- information that can be measured
- information that cannot be measured.

Information that can be measured is called **quantitative information**. A good example is the figures produced from a questionnaire. Quantitative information is always in exact numbers.

Information that cannot be measured is called **qualitative information**. A good example of qualitative information is the opinion of someone who you have interviewed. Qualitative

information is not exact but is a useful way of showing a trend, an idea or an opinion.

One way of presenting qualitative information

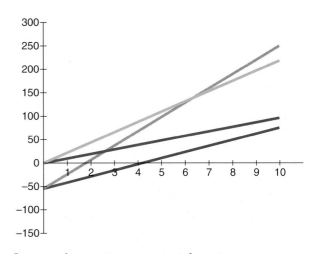

One way of presenting quantitative information

Hint

It is important that you know what type of information you want before you start your research. A questionnaire is good for getting answers to the same question from a lot of people but it is no good for finding out what one person really thinks about something.

Presenting information

The presentation of your results is an important stage in the design process. The type of graph or chart that is used can help to communicate the information. Some ways of drawing graphs are more suitable than others. Choose the type of graph carefully, according to the information that you are displaying.

Line graphs

The most common type of graph is the line graph. This is a set of crosses or dots which are joined together forming a line. The line graph is useful for showing changes over time.

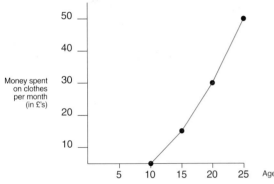

An example of a line graph

Bar charts

Sometimes it is useful to make a comparison of results. For example, one way of comparing the results of a questionnaire into your classmates' favourite colours is to draw a bar chart. A bar chart (histogram) enables you to quickly compare one item with another. It is very easy to see the biggest and smallest in any category.

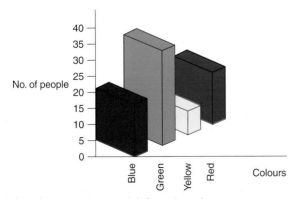

A bar chart showing people's favourite colours

Pie charts

Sometimes it is useful to present information as a percentage of the whole. This is particularly important if you want to use the information to make a decision. For example, if you found out that the favourite colour of 15 of the 100 people who answered your questionnaire was red, you might then suggest that 15 per cent of all people's favourite colour was red. This information can be clearly shown on a percentage pie chart.

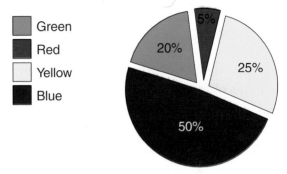

Pie chart showing people's favourite colours

Line graphs, bar charts and pie charts are usually two-dimensional (2-D). These charts can be made more interesting by using a computer to produce three-dimensional (3-D) graphs and charts. Computers can help you to present charts quickly and easily.

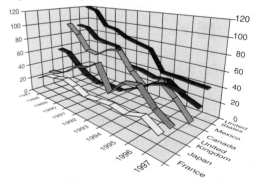

An example of a 3-D chart

To do

1. Produce a bar chart which represents your classmates' favourite colours.

2. Produce a percentage pie chart of the same results.

Charts, graphs and displays

Bringing information to life

So far we have looked at the standard graphs and charts used for presenting information. Bar charts, pie charts and line graphs form the basis of presentations, but graphic designers are always looking for ways to give their presentations impact. Often the theme of the research can be included in the design.

In the illustration below, the pie chart has been made into a plate showing the results of a survey of people's favourite snacks.

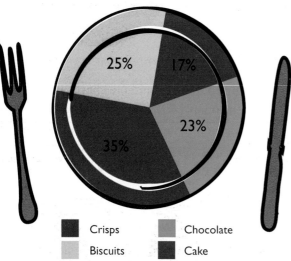

A pie chart made into a plate

Charts can have particular impact when they are used to communicate qualitative data. In this example, the design of the chart is used to create effect rather than give accurate results.

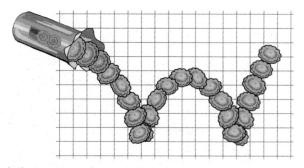

A chart using graphics to communicate qualitative data

Using pictograms

A **pictogram** is a graphic symbol that is used instead of words. It takes up less space and does not rely on people speaking the same language. Pictograms are often so well known that they are used all around the word.

The pictograms below are used in a camping brochure. Can you work out what each pictogram means?

Camping pictograms

Pictograms in graphs and charts

The simplest way of bringing a graph or chart to life is to add a pictogram. For example, pictograms have been used in the charts opposite to make them more relevant and interesting.

Pictograms can be used to represent the bars in a bar chart. This helps to communicate the results and create interest in them.

Pictograms bring a graph or chart to life and therefore add to the interest of a presentation.

SPECIFIC RESEARCH

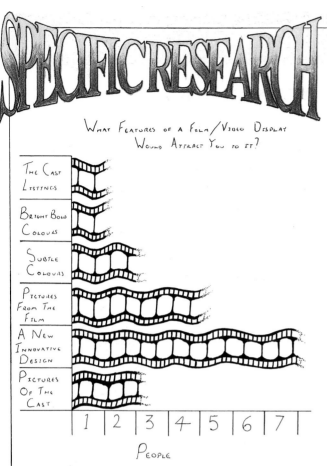

What Features of a Film/Video Display Would Attract You to it?

The Cast Listings
Bright Bold Colours
Subtle Colours
Pictures From The Film
A New Innovative Design
Pictures Of The Cast

1 2 3 4 5 6 7

People

Over the next couple of pages will be the results of my questionnaire.

This is the first set of results it shows the results to the question 'What Features of a Film/Video Display Would Attract You to it?'.

These results show that a new innovative design for a point and sell display would be a good way of attracting people to look at the videos so I will try and incorporate it in my design.

The second highest result was for the design to include pictures from the film, this 4 votes so I will try and include this in my design.

Although other subjects got votes but I don't think I will try and include them as they are obviously not as popular.

(A special offer on the display was also a choice but as it got no votes I decided not to include it.)

A pupil's pictogram showing the results of a survey into video

tea   coffee   hot chocolate

A pictogram is used here to show the favourite hot drinks of a sample of 60 people

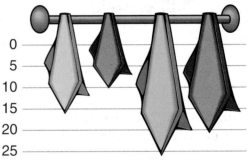

A pictogram is used to show the favourite tie colour of a sample of 70 people

To do

Design a pictogram bar chart to present this information:

Out of 30 pupils in a class, 15 have 20 or more CDs, 10 have between 10 and 20 CDs, and 5 have fewer than 10 CDs.

Learning from products

Looking carefully at products that are similar to the one you are going to design is an important part of the design process. To learn successfully from existing products you have to look at them with a 'critical eye'. Looking critically at products and asking questions about them is known as **product analysis**.

Analysing graphic products

When you analyse a product you should always use the 5WH approach (see page 9). This will act as a good starting point. A point of sale display is a graphic product so, for example, if you were

A point of sale display made from cardboard

analysing the **point of sale** display in the photo above, you might ask the following questions. (A point of sale display is used in shops and stores to hold leaflets and advertize new product.)

Who is the product aimed at?

To answer this question for the point of sale display, you have to think of the type of product it is promoting. For example, soap powder is usually aimed at adults. Look to see if there are any visual clues. A visual clue is anything that helps you to understand what the designer's intentions are. It may be a picture, a style of writing or a particular choice of colours. So, for example, the visual clues in the point of sale display above are the use of pictures with children's characters, together with bright colours and large lettering.

What is the purpose of the point of sale display?

The display has to hold leaflets, but how many? Does the number of leaflets it needs to hold affect its size? Leaflets are usually made to a standard size that could be A4, A5 or even A6.

Holding leaflets is probably the primary function (or main purpose) of the point of sale display. It will also have the secondary functions of attracting attention to the product being advertized on the leaflets, and helping to sell it.

What material has been used, and why?

Cardboard has been used to make the point of sale display on the left. This is the material that is usually used for point of sale displays. This is because:

- It is cheaper than plastic. This is important because usually point of sale displays only have to last for as long as the product promotion.
- It is easy to print onto. This helps to keep costs down.
- It can be folded flat for delivery. This is important for transportation and storage.

This point of sale leaflet holder is not made from cardboard. Can you think why?

Graphic products are often short-lived

Things like tickets and posters are designed to last for a short period of time before they are

A range of short-lived graphic products

The same basic product has been designed differently

thrown away. One of the most important questions for you to ask is how does the fact that many graphic products are short-lived affect their design and manufacture?

Comparing graphic products

Sometimes it is useful to compare graphic products to find out why similar products have been designed differently. A good example of this is chocolate wrappers. There are hundreds of types of chocolate bar that are all more or less the same and have the same function. However, their wrappers have all been designed differently.

Comparing products helps you to answer the question 'why?'

- **Why** are different colours used? Red is commonly used because it stands out. Think of other colours and what they do.
- **Why** do products aimed at children look different from products designed for teenagers or adults? Thinking about this question will help you to understand about different markets. A market is the type of people who use a certain product.
- **Why** do products have different types of packaging and use different materials? Thinking about this question will help you to understand about production and packaging techniques, and why some products have to be completely sealed.

To do

1 Collect examples of chocolate wrappers or use the photo above to compare different wrappers. Try to think of reasons why the designers have made them differently.

2 Be a graphic product detective by looking for visual clues that help you to discover the market for a product. For example, you could look at the same chocolate wrappers you used in question 1.

Design ideas

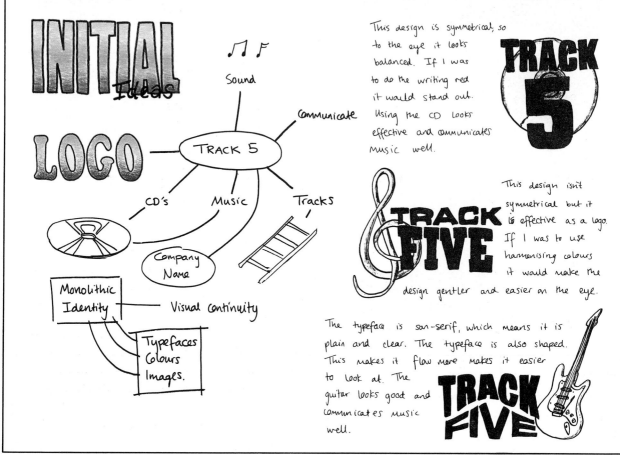

Use your research and brainstorm to help you come up with a variety of initial ideas

Design ideas are the first thoughts you have about a solution to your design problem. They are sometimes called rough ideas because they are incomplete solutions. You should always sketch these ideas rather than spend a long time carefully drawing them. Remember this motto:

'Designing is thinking on paper'

Think small then grow

It is often a good idea to break down a problem into smaller pieces and then bring the bits together as your ideas grow and develop. For example, when designing packaging for a new product, think about the style of writing you want, then consider the backgrounds, images and different colours.

To get you started, think about your research, look again at existing products and sketch any idea that comes into your head, even if it seems bizarre.

Choosing a design

The first idea you think of is rarely the best. When developing your idea you must always look back at your design specification (see page 9). The specification will give you all the **criteria** you need to judge how successful an idea is. Think about:

- Will it sell?
- Is it attractive?
- Does it fulfil its function?
- What will it cost?

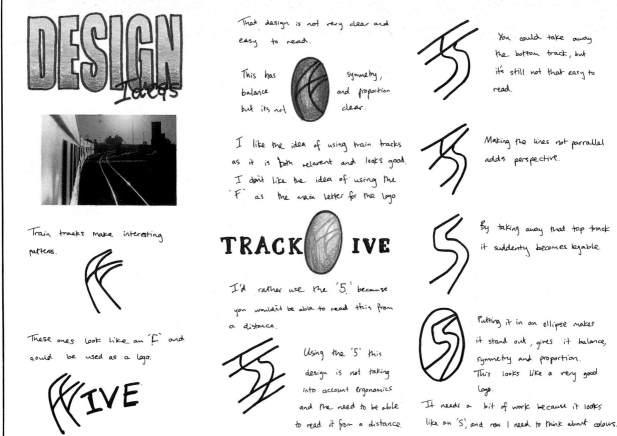

The drawings above show some design ideas for a logo

If you cannot decide, speak to somebody else. Often people find it hard to criticize their own ideas – others do so freely!

Communicating ideas

The word 'communicating' means using a language to explain something to somebody else. When you design you use a visual language. This means using pictures to communicate your ideas. It should help to explain your ideas both to yourself and others.

Always:

- use rough sketches and include notes
- ignore the tiny details – these will come later when you develop your ideas
- think small then grow
- come up with a wide range of ideas (a range is always three or more)
- use a blow up of a feature if you need to show more detail.

The best ideas are often scruffy little sketches – an idea is not improved by making it look good. So, don't reject an idea purely on appearance. These ideas might have a good feature that you can use somewhere else.

To do

1. Sketch three ideas for a new font to be used on the wrapper for the new chocolate bar 'Cruncher'.

2. Using a range of sketches with notes, design a 'do not disturb' sign for a hotel room (remember, a range is always three or more).

3. Sketch five different things you could do with a paper clip.

Development and final design

Developing an idea

The **development** of the design is a really important stage where the idea is gradually improved so the best design can be produced. To achieve the best possible solution you will need to:

- combine the best parts of your first ideas
- refine your ideas
- carry out more research
- make models or paper mock-ups to test your ideas
- evaluate your ideas against the specification.

Below is how the design idea for the logo shown on page 21 could have been developed. At this stage, graphic designers often use a computer to 'model' the idea. A model is used so that the designer can evaluate how good the idea is in reality.

Testing ideas

As designs develop it is good policy to test out the idea on a range of products. When designing a range of products that use the same logo it is important to see if the design will work.

Moving onto the computer I have decided to put coloured rings around the 5 to give it symmetry and colour and help it to stand out.

The colours here are good because they are bold, some compliment and most are primary colours.

The trouble with the last one was that the square writing stopped it looking curved so here I have curved the writing. It looks better.

The colours were a little too bold so here I have merged the yellow with red to make it easier on the eye.

So from these 4 components I have found my logo →

Ideas can be improved by using a computer to quickly change them

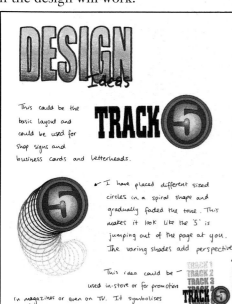

This could be the basic layout and could be used for shop signs and business cards and letterheads.

I have placed different sized circles in a spiral shape and gradually faded the tone. This makes it look like the '5' is jumping out of the page at you. The varing shades add perspective.

This idea could be used in-store or for promotion in magazines or even on TV. It symbolises how 'Track 5' stores stand out from the rest.

The above design could be used as one of these. They are stuck to the wall and they bounce. These could be given away free or stuck in-store.

Its printed on special plastic which absorbs the ink. This material is quite expensive so this may limit the number that can be produced.

The print process that could be used for these would be Flexography as this is good on thin, non-porous surfaces such as plastic. The ink is mixed with a solvent which enables the ink to dry quickly. It is a speedy process and suitable for large print runs.

A pupil's design ideas for a logo

Why this design?

It is important that each sketch is fully explained. The notes that are next to the sketch should say what the idea is and why you have decided to include it. Within design development, your notes must:

- describe your ideas
- explain your design
- evaluate how well your designs meet the specification

The final design

The final design should include a presentation drawing, and a working drawing that shows all the detail required to make the product.

The drawings opposite shows the finished design (the presentation drawing) and the net.

The working drawing

The working drawing on the right shows the shape of the package before it is made up. Dotted lines tell the manufacturer where folds are needed. Solid lines indicate cut lines. The most important thing to remember about any working drawing is that it should provide enough information for the product to be made.

The presentation drawing

The presentation drawing should be produced to the highest possible standard. This is because designers often have to 'sell' their idea to a client. Usually at this stage computer programs are used to produce the drawing. Realistic images can be scanned from photographs and added to the drawing.

To do

Find a piece of packaging and take it apart. Sketch a working drawing of the package to include all cut and fold lines, and measurements.

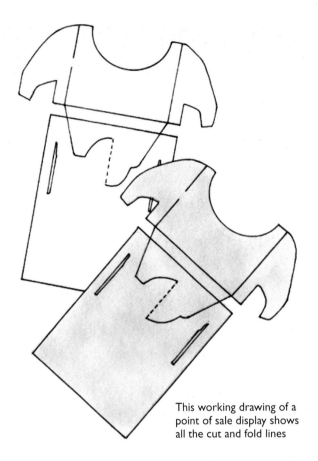

This working drawing of a point of sale display shows all the cut and fold lines

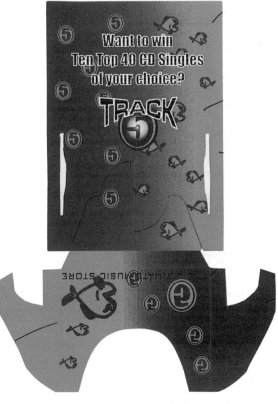

A presentation drawing showing a pupil's design solution

Planning the make

Having successfully designed your new graphic product, the next stage in the design process is to produce a step plan of how you are going to make it. A useful way of showing this plan is to use a **flow chart**.

Flow charts

Flow charts show the order that tasks must be done in. They show when decisions need to be taken and what the possible consequences of those decisions might be.

So that flow charts can be understood by everyone, standard symbols are used. The symbols have special shapes and show different activities.

Flow chart symbols

> START

An oval is used to show the start and end of a flow chart

> IS IT THE RIGHT FONT?

A diamond is used as a decision box

> MOVE LOGO TO TOP RIGHT

A rectangle is used to show an action – when a process is carried out

> PUT DESIRED PAPER INTO PRINTER

A parallelogram is used when something is put in or taken out

> HAPPY?

This shape is used for modifications or checking

Flow charts can become quite long and detailed if they represent the whole production process (make). It is a good idea to break down the make into smaller parts, called sub-sections. For example, a flow chart for scanning a picture might look like this:

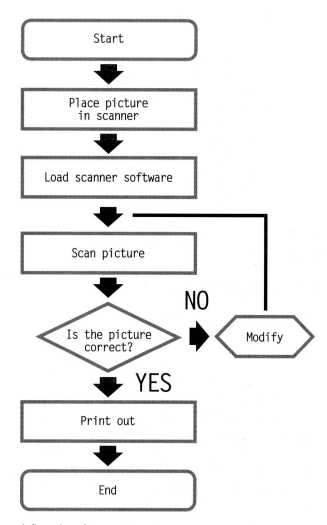

A flow chart for scanning a picture

Flow charts become more complicated when decisions and modifications need to be made. When these are included, the flow chart loops around. This is shown in the example on page 25 where a compliments slip is being produced.

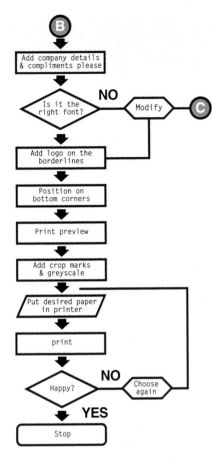

A flow chart for producing a compliments slip

Managing your time

Planning is important because it helps prevent mistakes and enables you to make good use of your time. Planning a Design and Technology project takes practice. It is always a good idea to write the stages down. When you allocate times to a process and state the equipment that is needed, your plan becomes a **production schedule**.

The production schedule opposite shows all the activities needed to make a compliments slip. The chart estimates the time needed for each stage and lists the tools and equipment likely to be needed. A schedule like this helps you to plan so that you do not run out of time or are not kept waiting for long periods for one stage to be completed.

As a checklist, your schedule should always include:

- each stage of the process in the correct order
- the time needed to complete each stage

- the tools, equipment and machinery needed
- any health and safety precautions.

The production schedule includes a visual plan of the product, which helps to communicate how you intend to create your product.

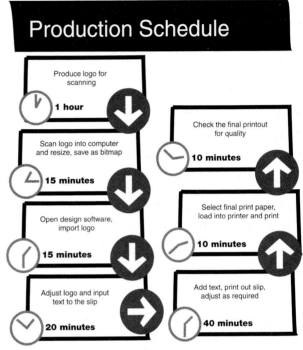

A production schedule to make a compliments slip

Hint

Look for things that take a long time and plan to work on a different task while you are waiting – this will ensure that you make good use of your time.

To do

1. Draw a flow chart for making a cup of tea.

2. Draw a production schedule for making sandwiches.

3. Draw a flow chart for preparing a bath of water. (Include decisions and details of tasks that can be completed while the water is running.)

Quality matters

What is quality?

We all know what we mean when we talk about quality, but it is hard to define. The Collins dictionary defines it as 'the mark or standard of excellence'. So, quality is about achieving the highest possible standards in all design activity.

Quality against cost

Achieving the highest quality often means having to spend more. For example, magazines are produced to a higher print quality than newspapers. The pictures are clearer, the paper is heavier, stronger and glossy. Magazines are usually in colour whereas newspapers are usually in black and white. The pictures in newspapers are not very crisp because the printing paper is not of as high a quality as those for a magazine. All this makes magazines more expensive to produce than newspapers.

'Glossy' colour magazines

Experiment

Take a magnifying glass and hold it over a newspaper picture. You will see that the picture is made up of a series of dots. If you do the same on a magazine it is virtually impossible to see the dots because they are so close together.

Quality control and quality assurance

When a large number of graphic products are being made it is important that the standard of quality is the same for each one. This is important because otherwise customers will be unhappy and the manufacturer will lose money. The customer expects to get good value for money from a quality product. In order to make money, the manufacturer must ensure that the products are made right first time so that there is no waste. In order to achieve quality the manufacturer uses **quality control** and **quality assurance** techniques.

Quality assurance

A statement of quality assurance (QA) is like a guarantee of quality written by the manufacturer. QA is a series of checks and procedures that takes place at every stage of production to ensure that goods are made correctly.

As part of the quality assurance programme there are a series of quality checks that are made to control the quality.

Quality control

Quality control is used to check that products meet the required quality standard. This means making a series of checks for things like colour and size. Graphic products that are printed have their quality controlled using a series of **printer's marks**.

In practice, quality control would be too time consuming if every product was individually inspected. In most systems a sample, such as 1 in every 100 products, is inspected. In this way the risk of failure of the production process is reduced. If the products are found to be acceptable, production is allowed to continue.

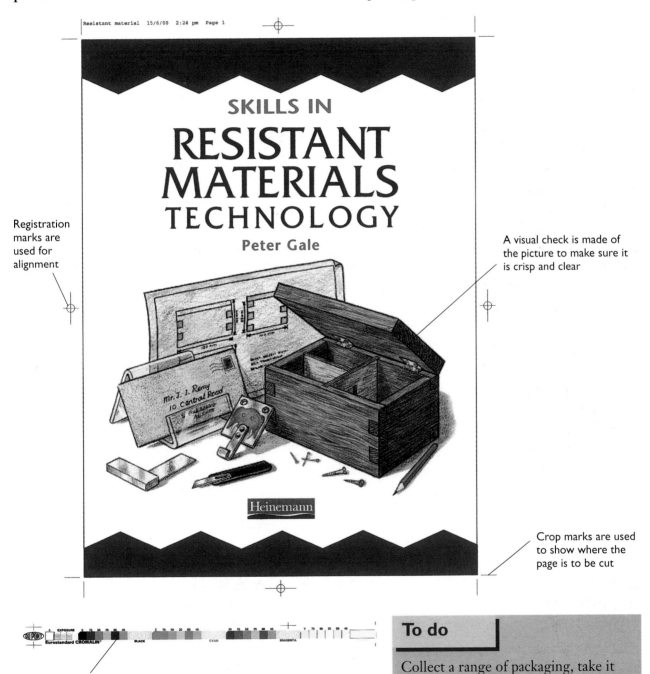

Registration marks are used for alignment

A visual check is made of the picture to make sure it is crisp and clear

Crop marks are used to show where the page is to be cut

Colour bars are used to check the colour in the picture

The front cover of a book showing printers marks

To do

Collect a range of packaging, take it apart and see if you can find examples of colour bars and crop marks.

Testing and evaluation

Testing

Testing a design solution is an important part of the design process. Before any products are manufactured they undergo a series of tests.

Physical tests

Physical tests are carried out to ensure that the design works according to the specification. For example, a leaflet holder will be tested to ensure that:

- It securely holds the right amount of leaflets
- It is stable (doesn't tip over easily)
- It is strong and rigid

A leaflet holder

Consumer tests

Consumer tests are carried out on a sample of people to find out which design they prefer from a range. (Sometimes these tests are called 'preference tests'.) This often helps designers improve the appearance of products. Decisions about the size of the text, what colours and graphic images to use can be influenced by what potential consumers think.

The results of consumer tests help designers to predict how popular products will be. They sometmes make changes to give their designs more impact or appeal.

> ### Tip
>
> *You can carry out consumer tests on your own designs by giving a questionnaire to your classmates. This is a good way of evaluating your designs.*

Prototypes

Prototypes are fully working products that are used for testing. They are carefully made to ensure that they are as close as possible to the final design. Once all tests have been completed and modifications made to the prototype designs, the finished product will be manufactured. Prototypes are often tested to destruction, particularly where safety is concerned.

This prototype of a car is being tested to destruction

Evaluation

Evaluation means critically asking questions about how well the ideas or final product meet the design specification. Many people assume that evaluation only occurs at the end of a project, when everything has been finished. In fact there are two main types of evaluation and these should be carried out in any design and technology project:

- formative evaluation
- summative evaluation.

Formative evaluation

Formative evaluation is ongoing. This means that it should be carried out throughout the project. Your research should be evaluated to judge how useful it is to your brief. Your ideas should be evaluated. This should be done by writing down your ideas and then making notes by the side of them. In fact, almost every page of your project should contain your evaluative notes.

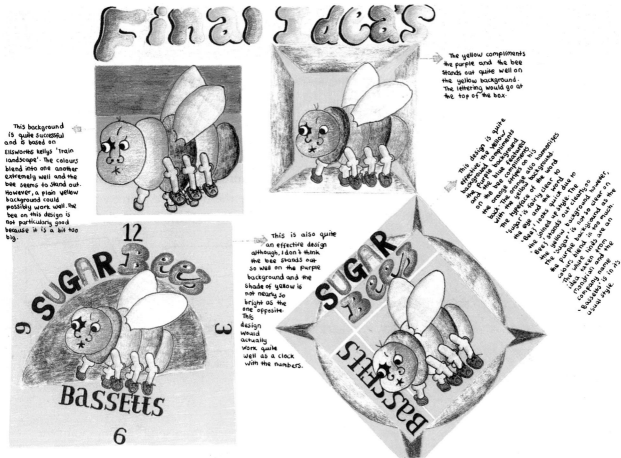

Examples of a pupil's formative evaluation

Summative evaluation

Summative evaluation occurs at the end of a project. It involves judging how well the final made product meets the specification drawn up at the beginning of the project.

Good evaluations should:

- Answer every point on the specification
- Be written in the third person (never say I think this or that)
- Be detailed
- Suggest improvements or recommendations with sketches.

Good evaluations should not:

- Be a diary of how well you got on during the project
- Just be your opinion.

When you have finished your final evaluation ask one more question:

'Does my final design meet the specification?'

Questions

Look back at the specification for the CD inlay on page 9.

1 What two physical tests could be carried out on the product?

2 What type of consumer test would you carry out for this product?

To do

Write a short evaluation of your last piece of written work at school. What were your intentions (the specification) and did you meet them?

Drawing

Practice makes perfect

If you were an athlete you would need to train regularly to prepare for events. The same is true for designers. Being able to draw and sketch quickly and accurately takes a good deal of practice. But, just like riding a bike, once you have learned, you never forget.

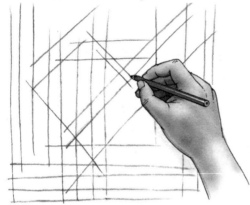

Practise drawing vertical, horizontal and diagonal lines. Always keep your hand to one side so that you can see the point of the pencil

Start simple and ghost lines

Before you start sketching, move the pencil backwards and forwards over the line you want to draw without touching the paper. Then, when you are ready, draw the line. It is a good idea to draw the line very faint at first. This is called ghosting, and the lines are called ghost or *feint* lines. When you have ghosted the sketch you can make any alterations before you go over it boldly.

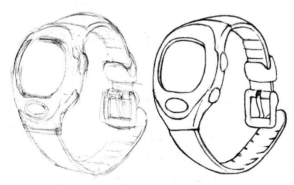

A ghosted sketch of a watch and a bold watch

Simple boxes

A good way to start drawing actual forms is to begin by sketching boxes. Use the ghosting technique and never draw the line boldly until you are sure it is right. When you draw a box, start with the front face. Once you have that correct the rest of the box is much easier to draw.

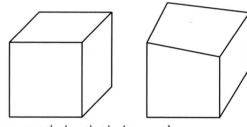

Can you spot the box that looks wrong?

Crates

Drawing boxes is a useful starting point for drawing complex things. Think of a box like a crate. A crate is something that goes around the outside of a product when it is being delivered to keep it safe. In the same way, a crate is used to enclose a drawing.

1 Start off by finding out all the sizes you need. Then draw a box the correct size.

2 Decide which of the three faces of the object go on each face of the crate.

3 Find the points where each face touches the box.

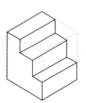

4 Draw each face in turn by joining the points.

Getting the proportion right

There is a saying used by designers – 'If it looks right, it is right'. This is not always true but when it is applied to a drawing it usually is. What this saying is referring to is **proportion**. Getting things in the right proportion is very important.

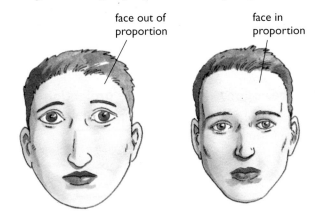

face out of proportion · face in proportion

When elements of a drawing are out of proportion the drawing looks wrong

Always get the proportions of the crate right, otherwise the drawing will be wrong.

The proportions of the crate depend upon the shape you want

Making drawings stand out

To make a drawing stand out, designers use a variety of techniques to show the form of the object. The form is the object's three-dimensional shape. One simple way of doing this is to use the thick and thin line technique.

Take a look at the drawings at the top-right of the page. You will see that by making some lines thick while keeping the others thin, the form of the object is clearly defined.

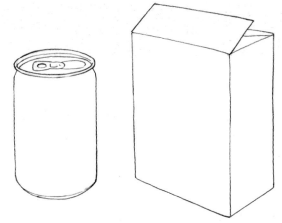

The form of these objects is clearly defined by using the thick and thin line technique

Applying the thick and thin line technique

A simple way of applying thick and thin lines is to imagine a spider walking over the object.

If a spider crosses over an edge and you can still see it, leave the line thin. If the spider disappears, draw the line about twice as thick.

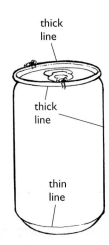

thick line · thick line · thin line

To do

1 Copy the two drawings and apply the thick and thin line technique.

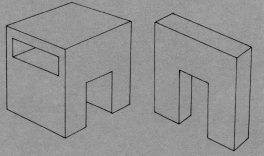

2 Using crates, sketch three common household objects. Measure them first and think carefully about the proportions. Apply the thick and thin line technique to your completed drawings.

Drawing in 3-D

Pictorial drawing

Pictorial is the name given to drawings that are in three dimensions. **Pictorial drawings** are popular with designers as a means of explaining an idea to a client. This is because they resemble the appearance of a product and are realistic.

It is hard to tell what this product is because the 2-D drawing does not give enough information

If the brick is now drawn in 3-D it is obvious what it is. The details of the brick are more clearly communicated.

The 3-D drawing represents bricks more clearly than the 2-D one

Three of the most useful pictorial drawing methods are:

- oblique projection
- isometric projection
- perspective (see pages 34–5).

Oblique projection

This is the easiest method of pictorial drawing. It is often the way that children and less experienced pupils begin to draw naturally. With oblique projection, the front face of the object is drawn as a true 'front view' (in 2-D).

Stages of drawing in oblique projection

1 The front face of the object is drawn as a true view.

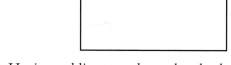

2 Horizontal lines are then taken back at 45 degrees.

3 The drawing is completed by adding the depth.

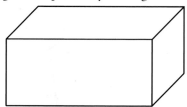

Circles are drawn in the same way. Be careful to ensure that the centre for a circle is moved along the 45 degree axis.

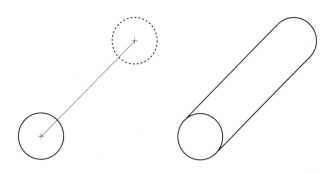

Circles in oblique

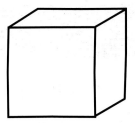

A simple oblique cube

Isometric projection

Isometric projection is very popular because it gives a more natural effect than oblique projection. With this method of pictorial drawing, all lines are taken back 30 degrees to the horizontal. Unlike oblique projection, all lines are drawn to scale.

Examples of isometric drawings

A useful way of sketching in isometric projection is to use a grid. Isometric grids can be laid underneath your paper and act as a guide for inserting your lines.

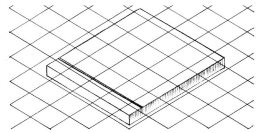

Using an isometric grid is a quick way of sketching

Hint

Isometric drawings can look a bit odd because your eye expects to see lines getting smaller as they go into the distance. Isometric drawings 'appear' to be getting bigger along their length.

Exploding your drawing

A photograph gives a good representation of a final product

A photograph or a drawing of a finished product gives a good representation but it does not give any assembly instructions. Isometric projection can be used to show how the different parts fit together.

A drawing that shows all the different parts of an object separated is called an exploded drawing. When producing an exploded isometric drawing, both the top and bottom parts should lie on the same vertical line.

An exploded isometric drawing of a CD case.

To do

Using the 'crate' method (see page 30) sketch three common household products in:

   a oblique projection

   b isometric projection.

Apply thick and thin lines to your drawings.

Perspective drawing

Take a look out of the window and look carefully at the view. You will notice that objects near to you appear to be much larger than objects in the distance. This is because your eye puts things into **perspective**. This means that as things get further away they get smaller (or diminish) until they eventually vanish.

Perspective enables you to create the most realistic drawings. The most common types of perspective drawing are single point perspective and two point perspective.

Objects such as a train appear to diminish into the distance

Vanishing points and horizon lines

All perspective drawings have a horizon line. The horizon line separates the sky from the ground and helps to position the view of the object. The horizon line is the line of sight.

The **vanishing point** or points are usually situated on the horizon line. This is the point where all the lines meet on your drawing.

Single point perspective

Sketching a CD case in single point

1 Draw a horizon line with a vanishing point at one end. Ghost a vertical line to represent the front edge of the cassette case.

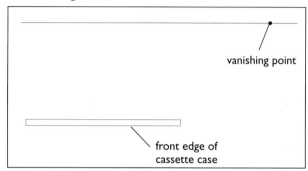

vanishing point

front edge of cassette case

2 Now, ghost lines from the front corners back to the vanishing point. Measure the length of the case and insert a vertical line for the back edge. Draw the horizontal back edge of the case.

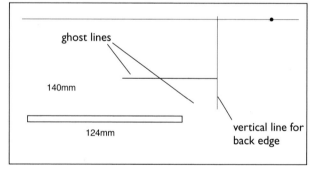

ghost lines

140mm

124mm

vertical line for back edge

3 Now, add the other details of the case, such as the thickness of the plastic and the hinges. Remember that all lines should go back to the vanishing point.

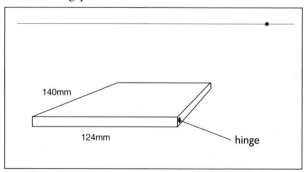

140mm

124mm

hinge

Two point perspective

Sketching a CD case in two point

1 Draw a horizon line with vanishing points at each end. Ghost a vertical line down to represent the front edge of the CD case.

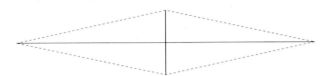

2 Now ghost lines from the front corners to the vanishing points. Then mark in the length of the sides.

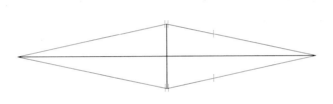

3 Draw in the other edges and add the detail remembering to take all lines back to the vanishing points.

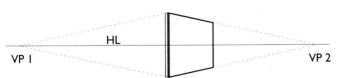

Above or below the line?

When constructing a perspective drawing, the object can be drawn either above, below or on the horizon line. If the object is drawn above the line, the underneath is shown. If the object is drawn below the horizon line the top surface is seen. If the object is drawn exactly on the horizon line, only the front surface is seen.

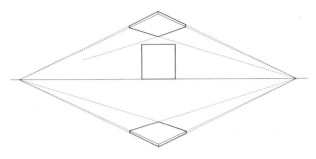

Objects above, below and on the horizon line

Creating interest

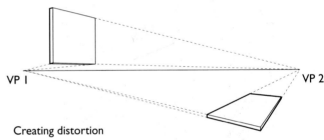

Creating distortion

Interesting distortions can be created by positioning the drawing very close to one of the vanishing points. The closer the object is to a vanishing point, the more distorted it will become. This may be unrealistic but it will add interest to your graphics.

To do

1 Draw a single point perspective of a stapler in the closed position. Add thick and thin lines.

2 Draw a two point perspective drawing of an open match box, above and below the horizon line.

Drawing circles and ellipses

Ellipses

An ellipse is a flattened circle. Imagine you are looking directly at someone sipping a can of fizzy drink. Look carefully at the shape of the bottom of the can.

1 Initially, only a very thin, flattened circle (ellipse) will be seen.

2 As more and more of the drink is consumed, the ellipse will become fatter.

3 As the can is brought to the horizontal, the full shape of the circle is seen.

Axes and touch points

If you draw a square, then a circle that fits exactly inside it, you will notice that it touches the square in four places. Also, the circle has a vertical and a horizontal axis which are equal in length.

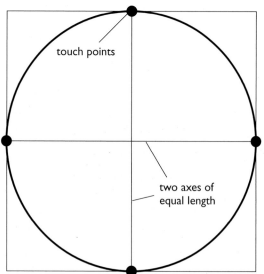

touch points

two axes of equal length

Because the ellipse is flattened, one axis is longer than the other. The longer axis is called the major axis and the shorter is called the minor axis.

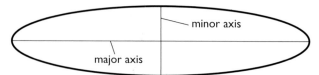

minor axis

major axis

Sketching an ellipse

Below is an ideal way for quickly sketching relatively small ellipses. Accurate drawings take a little more time and effort.

1 First, ghost the crate for the ellipse in isometric projection. Find the centre of the crate by joining the diagonals.

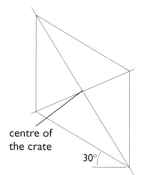

centre of the crate

30°

2 Draw in the two axes to find the four touch points.

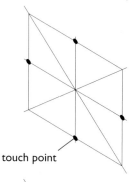

touch point

3 Carefully join the four touch points with curves. Ghost the curves first until you get a curve that looks right.

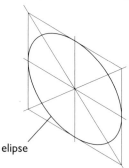

elipse

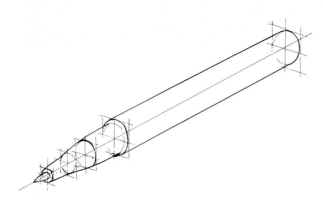

By repeating the ellipse construction it is possible to produce more complex objects

More accurate curves

To produce more accurate curves you need more touch points on your circle. This is relatively easy to do but you need a pair of compasses to divide the square into equal slices.

1 Draw a line at any angle to the square and use a pair of compasses to mark off six equal divisions.

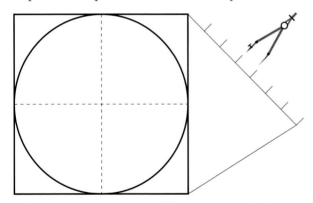

2 Join the bottom edge of the square to the last mark on the angled line. Next, join all the other marks on the line to the square with parallel lines.

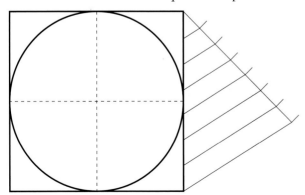

3 Now draw parallel lines across the box. The new touch points are where these lines cross the circle.

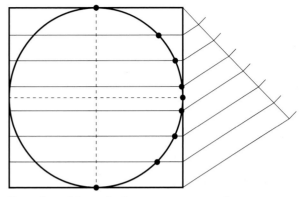

By using this technique you can produce accurate drawings. The drawing of the CD and case below shows how touch points have been used to create the shape of the CD and its holder.

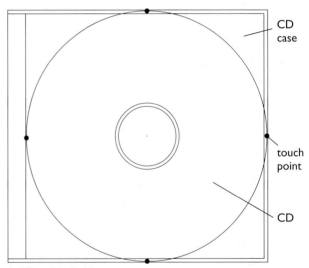

A CD and its holder

To do

The drawing below shows the front and side view of a battery. Find out the dimensions of a battery and, using isometric projection, produce an accurate drawing.

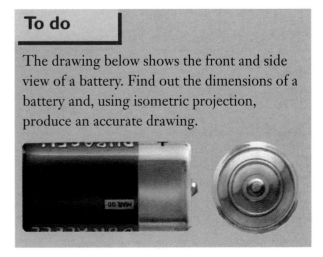

Orthographic drawing part 1

What is an orthographic drawing?

An orthographic drawing is a working drawing designed to provide all the information needed to make a product. It is used by professionals such as engineers and architects. Being able to understand and draw orthographic drawings is a vital skill for the designer.

Unlike pictorial drawing which always gives three dimensions, orthographic drawings view objects 'flat on'. That means they show each face in turn and are therefore two-dimensional.

Plans and elevations

Orthographic drawings have a language all of their own. A view looking down on the object from above is called the plan. A view of either the front or the end is called an **elevation**.

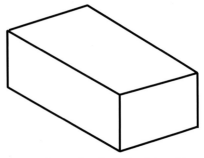

When drawing orthographically, think of the object as a folded-up box

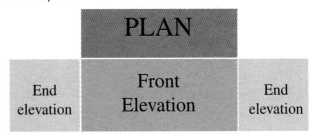

The four main orthographic views

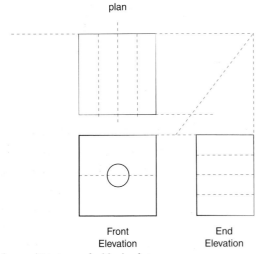

Orthographic views of a block of steps

Unfolding the box

The best way to understand the layout of an orthographic drawing is to think of the object as a folded-up box. As the box is unfolded, and laid out flat, each of the sides end up in the correct position.

This type of layout is known as third angle orthographic projection. With third angle, the view is drawn from where the eye is looking. There is a standard symbol that should appear on every drawing. This symbol shows that it is a third angle orthographic projection rather than any other type of orthographic drawing.

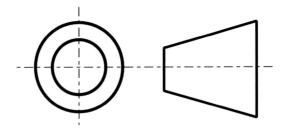

The symbol for third angle orthographic projection

The symbol shows an end elevation and front view of a cone with the top removed – the shape is like a lampshade. When you look into the cone you see a small circle which is the hole in the top and a large circle which is the bottom edge.

Orthographic drawing in action

When all the different views come together, an orthographic drawing is produced. Orthographic drawings are precise, include dimensions (measurements) and are drawn to scale.

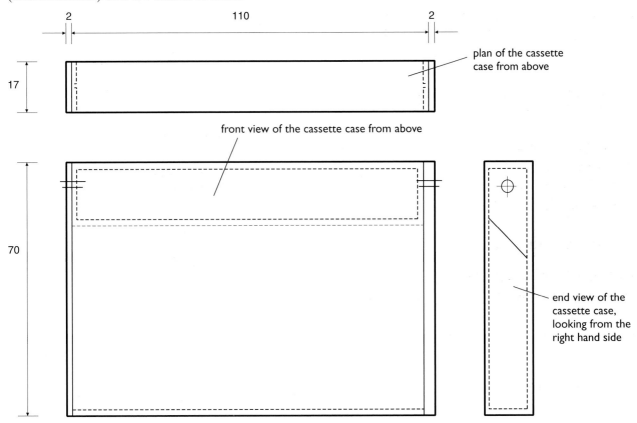

An orthographic drawing of a cassette box

The **scale** that the drawing uses must always be shown. In the drawing above, the scale used is 1:2. This means that the drawing is drawn half full size. Dimensions are always shown in millimetres.

Line types

Orthographic drawings are carefully drawn with either a hard pencil (4H) or a fine line pen. The feint (ghost) lines used to lay out the drawing are called construction lines. The other line types used are:

A centre line ▬ · ▬ · ▬ · ▬ · ▬ · ▬ · ▬ ·
(which shows the centre of a circle)

Hidden detail ▬ ▬ ▬ ▬ ▬ ▬ ▬ ▬ ▬ ▬ ▬ ▬
(which shows detail that can't be seen)

Hidden detail must be included on the drawing. The drawing above shows an orthographic drawing of a cassette case. The small pivots that connect the two halves of the case together cannot be seen on the front elevation, but must be shown as hidden detail.

To do

Look carefully at three objects that you have in your pencil case, such as a pencil sharpener, pencil and ruler.

For each object, draw a plan, front elevation and end elevation using third angle orthographic projection.

Orthographic drawing part 2

Producing an orthographic drawing

The best way of producing an orthographic drawing is to use a drawing board with either a T square or a parallel motion rule. If you use this equipment, all lines will be straight and the top and bottom edges can be drawn at right angles to one another.

Drawing board and equipment

Planning the drawing

The first task is to decide which face will be the front elevation. This will determine all the other views. Usually the front elevation is the view that shows the most detail of the object. Consider the object below:

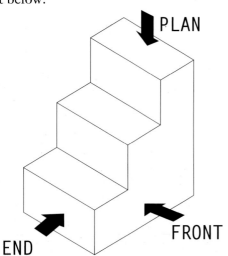

Stage 1 Plan the page

You need to ensure that there is enough room for all the views. It is usual to draw the front elevation in the middle of the page but be careful that there is room for the plan.

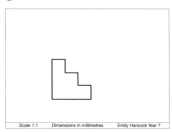

The front elevation is drawn first

Stage 2 Construct the end elevation

Using the parallel rule and a 4H pencil, draw lines from each point on the front elevation towards the end elevation and the plan.

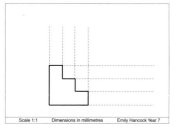

Construction lines drawn for end elevation and plan

Stage 3 Pencil in the end elevation

Carefully go over the end elevation with a 2H pencil.

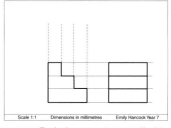

End elevation is pencilled in

Stage 4 Construct the plan

From a point exactly halfway between the front and end elevation, draw a construction line at 45 degrees. When the construction lines from the end elevation hit the 45 degree line, draw horizontal construction lines.

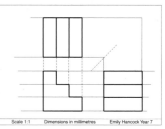

The plan is constructed using a 45 degree line

The final drawing

The final drawing includes all the dimensions (measurements). The dimensions are needed in order to make the object. In the final drawing, a second end elevation is often added to make the drawing clearer

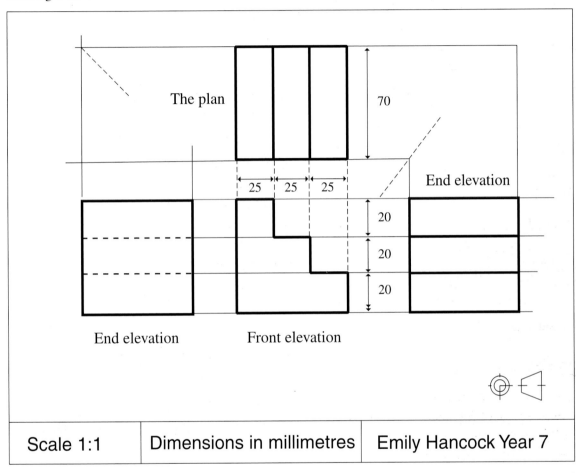

The plan

70

End elevation

25   25   25

20

20

20

End elevation   Front elevation

Scale 1:1	Dimensions in millimetres	Emily Hancock Year 7

Completed orthographic drawing

To do

Look carefully at the pictorial drawings below.
For each object produce a complete orthographic drawing.

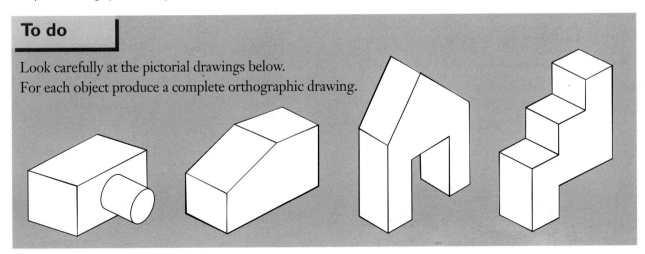

Light and shade

Into the shade

One effective way of making an object look realistic is to apply shading to it. If this shading is to look true to life, the effect of light must be taken into account. When light falls on an object, surfaces reflect different amounts of light, depending upon their position in relation to the light. The rule is:

- horizontal surfaces reflect more light than vertical surfaces
- surfaces nearest the light source reflect more light.

The more light is reflected, the lighter is the surface.

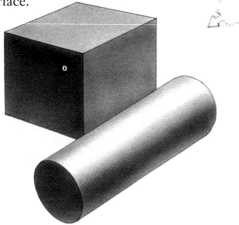

The effect of light on different surfaces

Using a pencil to shade

A soft pencil such as a 2B is ideal for producing a range of tones. By applying differing amounts of pressure on the pencil, **tonal shading** is produced. It is called tonal shading because one colour is used and the form of an object is shown through the tonal differences.

A tonal range card produced by shading with a 2B pencil

Shading regular forms

Using a soft lead pencil it is easy to make 3-D forms come to life. Remember the light rule and apply the tones to suit.

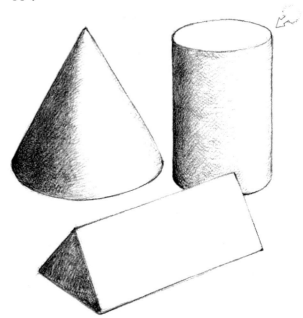

A range of regular forms shaded using a soft pencil

Putting the object in a box

When you have drawn a more complex object, it is best to think of it as a cube. In that way the different light surfaces can easily be identified.

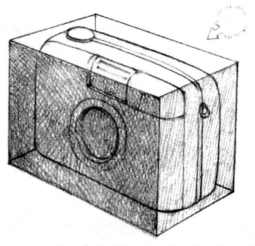

Using a crate to identify the different surfaces for reflected light

Line shading

An alternative and much quicker way of shading an object is to use lines. By varying the number of lines, their thickness and their spacing, shading can be achieved.

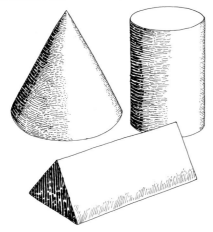

Line shading of regular forms

Using coloured paper

We tend to think that white paper is all we can use for graphic products. In fact, some of the best results can be achieved by using coloured paper as a background. Black sugar paper and a white pencil is particularly effective.

When using this method you have to work in reverse but otherwise the toning is the same as for a normal pencil. Highlights are emphasized with solid white.

Using black sugar paper and a white pencil

When working with coloured paper it is best to use the 'rougher', more textured surface. This side will take colour more easily.

All wrapped up

The sketches below were drawn on brown packaging paper. This is particularly good for rendering. It has a heavily textured surface which is good for both pencils and marker pens. Another advantage of this paper is that both white and black pencils can be used.

The drawing of the pen shows how a marker pen and black and white pencils can be used. The whisk of white, drawn diagonally across the pen, shows the direction of the light.

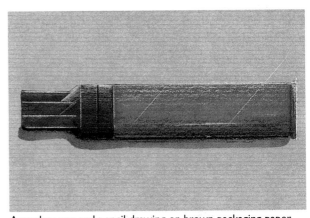

A marker pen and pencil drawing on brown packaging paper

To do

1. Draw a rectangle and, using a 2B pencil, produce a seven-tone range.

2. Produce a range of designs for a bracelet display using black sugar paper and a white pencil.

Using colour

Why use colour?

Colour is used to bring a drawing to life. It can make a particular part of a drawing stand out, make it look more attractive, or help communicate details about the object being shown, such as the material it's made from.

A drawing's too flat without it

Colour is usually added to a drawing to show its form (its three-dimensional shape). By using different tones or shades of colour, the form can be shown. Compare the two drawings of the mouse below. Colour helps to show the curves and rounded corners. Often colour is the main clue you have about an object's shape.

A flat and a rendered drawing of a mouse

Clues about the material

Often as designers we need to visually communicate detail, like the material an object is made from. When colour is evenly applied to an object, it does not give any clues about this.

Flat colour gives no clue about the material an object is made from

Reflections or surface detail can be seen in most plastics, metals or painted surfaces. Very shiny materials, such as glass or chrome, actually reflect pictures of an object near to them. This is difficult to show on a drawing so it is best to use reflections that have no recognizable shape. Reflections drawn to show shiny surfaces should run diagonally to contrast with horizontal and vertical lines.

When the material is non-reflective, like wood, surface details should be shown. With wood you should choose a colour which is similar to the object's colour, then draw the wood grain over it.

Reflections drawn at 45 degrees with no recognizable shape. A pencil or marker can be used. This is a good way of showing acrylic

A common way of showing a metallic surface like steel. Light blue stripes are drawn with a little grey added

When coloured pencil is used the tone can be varied. The effect of light and dark lines helps to show reflections

Dark brown lines are used to indicate the grain over a lighter brown background

Rounded edges

When light falls on a rounded surface that is facing the light, it will reflect light towards the eye. When light falls on a surface facing away from the light, it will reflect light away from the edge.

The part of the surface facing the light reflects the most light. The curved surface reflects the light away

Reflected light is shown as a white line. This is known as highlighting. By making the edges of the lettering white it gives the impression they are rounded or bevelled (sloping).

Curves and rounded edges with added highlight and shadow

Using colour as a background

A simple yet effective way of making your drawings stand out is to use colour as a background. This has the effect of 'lifting' the object off the page. This is especially effective when used with thick and thin lines.

Background colour makes objects stand out

Bringing it together

When presenting design sketches it is a good idea to combine some of these techniques. You should try to use colour for a purpose. When used carefully it will improve your work.

The following sketches show the first designs for a desk tidy. A range of different materials have been considered.

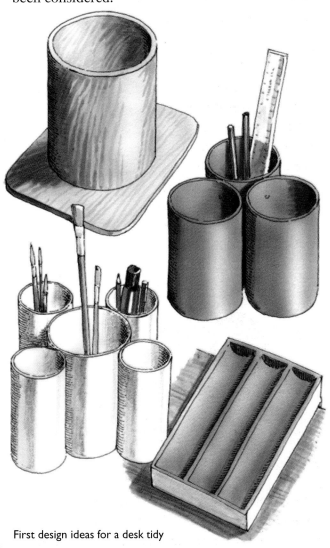

First design ideas for a desk tidy

To do

Using a range of sketches with notes, design a fold-up desk tidy. Consider different materials and use a range of colour effects to emphasize your work.

Effective colour techniques

Putting things in the shadow

Objects that have been shaded or rendered will look even more realistic if a shadow is added. All objects that face a light source will cast a shadow. Think carefully about the direction of the light and its position in relation to the object. Applying a shadow to a two-dimensional sketch helps to make it look more three-dimensional.

The colour of the shadow is always darker than the colour of the surface on which it falls. On a red object, the shadow will be a darker red. When drawing on white paper, shadow can be added using a soft lead pencil.

Applying shadow to two-dimensional shapes

Text shadows

Shadows are also a good way of making headings more dynamic. Using a 'drop shadow' on text helps to give it the impression of movement and makes it stand out from the page. Shadow writing is often used in magazines and newspapers to create impact.

Mixing media

As we saw on page 43 with the rendered pen, it is possible, and indeed sometimes advisable, to mix different **media** together. Marker pens often need a pencil to apply tone and give the drawing depth. Pencil drawings can be improved by using a marker pen to provide a background. As with all design drawings, you must be careful not to 'overdo' your work with too many combinations. Colours should always work well together and it is better to use too few colours and media combinations than too many.

Remember: You can always add but it is much harder to take away.

Avoid mistakes

However good you are at adding colour to a drawing, it will never look good unless the drawing itself is right. Take your time and experiment first. This is especially important when using a marker pen. Marker pens cannot be erased once they have been applied.

Hint

Take a photocopy of your drawing and render that. If you make any mistakes you've still got your original drawing.

A close shave

A good exercise is to produce a rendered drawing of a disposable razor. It is relatively simple to draw but looks very effective when it has been completed.

A disposable razor

Stage 1

Make a 2-D pencil drawing of the razor. It is a good idea to draw the view from above. Don't put too much detail onto the sketch because it will not be seen when it is rendered.

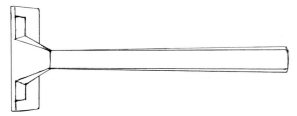

The drawing needs to be crisp so that the lines show through when the drawing is photocopied

Stage 2

Using a marker pen, render the photocopy. Take care to ensure an even covering.

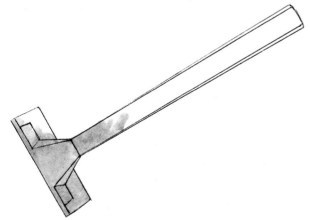

Rendered drawing of a razor

Stage 3

Using a black and white pencil, apply light and dark tones to the drawing to emphasize its features.

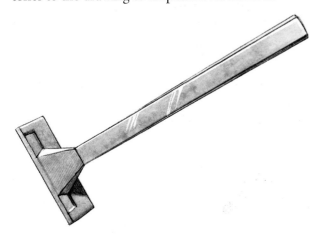

Drawing of a razor with light and dark tones added

Stage 4

Cut out your drawing and mount it. It is virtually impossible to keep within the lines when using a marker pen. Graphic designers usually cut around the rendered object using a craft knife or scalpel.

Cutting around the rendered razor

Objects that are difficult to render, such as the shiny razor blades, can be replaced on the drawing by silver foil. To achieve this, small slots are cut into the drawing where the blades would be and the silver foil is glued onto the back.

The final drawing can then be mounted onto a coloured background using glue.

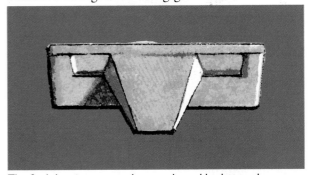

The final drawing mounted on a coloured background

To do

Sketch six designs for a new ball point pen. Produce a final presentation drawing and render it with a marker pen. Using a black and a white pencil, add tone to the drawing.

Using a craft knife, cut out your final drawing and mount it on a coloured background.

Colour in focus

Colour is very important to the designer. It affects the way products look, how we feel about them and how we react to them. Different colours can mean different things to us. For example, if we see red we recognize danger – red means stop and green means go. Black is heavy and yellow is light. Colour communicates and informs us about products. In nature, yellow and black stripes are found on wasps, bees and certain snakes. In factories, yellow and black stripes are used as warnings on dangerous machines.

Different colours communicate different things

Colour theory

If we want to use colour to improve the appearance of a product or to help communicate information, we need to understand some basic principles of colour theory.

Primary colours

In design work the **primary colours** are red, yellow and blue. They are called primary colours (first colours) because they are the only colours that cannot be created by mixing other colours together.

The primary colours

Secondary colours

The three colours produced by mixing each of the three primary colours together are called **secondary colours** (second colours).

Secondary colours
• yellow + blue = green
• yellow + red = orange
• blue + red = purple

The secondary colours

The colour wheel

The best way of showing how the primary and secondary colours work together is to make a colour wheel. The colour wheel makes up the colours of the rainbow. If you start from red and follow the colours round anti-clockwise they follow the pattern of the colours of the rainbow.

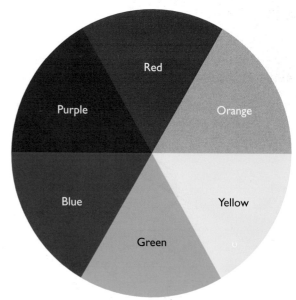

The colour wheel

A rainbow has the same colours as the colour wheel

Using colour in design

Complementary colours

Have you ever noticed that some colours work well together and some don't? Colours that are opposite each other on the colour wheel create contrast and improve the appearance of both colours. These colours are called **complementary colours**.

Complementary colours

- *orange complements blue*
- *red complements green*
- *yellow complements purple*

Blue and orange are opposites on the colour wheel – they complement one another

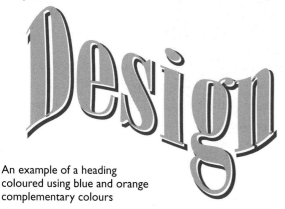
An example of a heading coloured using blue and orange complementary colours

Harmonizing colours

Colours that are neighbours on the colour wheel are called **harmonizing colours**. This means that they are in harmony with one another.

Yellow and green are neighbours on the colour wheel – they harmonize with one another

Blending colours with a pencil

Colours that harmonize, such as blue and green can be blended together to give pleasing effects – this can only be achieved with neighbours on the colour wheel.

Blue and green are harmonizing colours – they blend together well

Hue and tone

The actual colour, such as blue or red, is called the **hue**. The hue can be changed by adding tone. The tone is the amount of light and dark (i.e. the amount of black or white) used.

100% – 0% tone

The effect of adding tone to hue

To do

1. Draw a small rectangle and choose two harmonizing colours. Render the box by blending the two colours together.

2. Write the word 'Design' using bubble writing. Colour this in using two complementary colours.

3. Collect different cuttings which show the use of colour in nature. Look for yellow and black stripes for warnings, red for danger and blue and white for crispness.

Point of sale displays

Attracting the customer

Next time you go into a bank, supermarket or video shop, look carefully at the way new products are introduced to the customer. They often use specially designed displays that advertize the product. These displays are nearly always made from card and are relatively cheap because they only need to last for the length of the promotion. They often hold leaflets and use bright bold colours to attract attention.

At the cash desk

The term **point of sale** means the place at which goods are sold. Everyone who buys something in a shop must pay at the cash desk or counter, and it is here that point of sale displays are usually found.

People often have to wait to be served. While they are waiting, they are a **captive** audience. A point of sale display on the counter gives people something to read and, hopefully, buy.

A point of sale display

At the cinema

Point of sale displays at the cinema

When a new film or video is launched, special displays are produced. Point of sale displays for films or new videos are often large cardboard cutouts that show characters or events from the film. They are designed to attract customers and are always placed in prominent positions. When you go to the cinema, large displays stand in the foyer.

Another common use of a point of sale display is to advertize **promotions** or price reductions.

A successful display?

A point of sale display might simply be a special arrangement of the products themselves, placed in a special case. More usually, point of sale displays involve posters, stickers and signs.

To be successful, point of sale displays must attract customers. Where they are placed can be as important as their design. Think about the displays you have seen. Ask yourself these questions:

- Where are they placed (position, height)?
- How do they attract and interest customers?
- How long do they last before they are replaced?

Attracting attention

One way that point of sale displays attract attention is to use slogans. Slogans are headlines that are short, snappy and make you look twice. Often the slogan holds some form of intrigue or clue to make the customer think. Look carefully at the display below to see how the designer has used a slogan to attract attention.

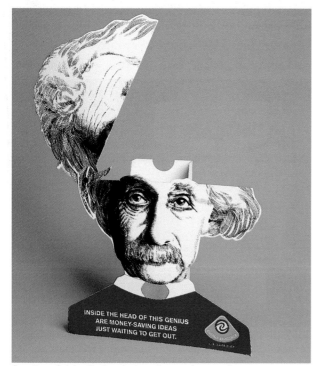

A point of dale display designed to grab attention

Key features of point of sale displays

When designing and making a point of sale display, you must make sure that it:

- **is interesting and eye-catching** to attract attention
- **is cheap to produce** because it has a short life and is then thrown away
- **is strong** because it is often pushed and knocked
- **can be flat packed** because it will probably be posted to the shops that will use it
- **clearly links to the product** so that the customer is left in no doubt
- **is easy to print** to keep the cost down

Often these displays involve complex nets, folds and cutouts. It is important that, when the display is folded into its correct shape, all the printing is in the right place. One of the key features of point of sale displays is that they should be easy to print and hence cheap to produce. To keep the cost of production down, they should be printed on one side only.

Twisting and turning

To achieve one-sided printing, a display often has a special turning joint which allows it to be turned before folding.

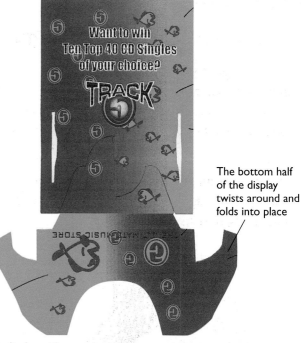

The bottom half of the display twists around and folds into place

A display with a turning joint

Research

Take a close look at a range of point of sale displays. Visit local shops and stores and make a list of the different examples you see.

Look out for:
- clever ideas
- slogans
- interesting graphics
- how they have been made.

Nets (developments)

The story unfolds

A net, or development, as it is often called, is the flat shape of a package or display stand that has been unfolded. Nets can be complicated to design, especially if they are unusual shapes. Some common shapes and their nets are shown below:

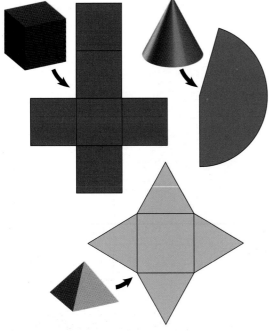

A range of common forms and their nets

Cut and fold lines

When nets are designed, the fold lines (which are always shown as dotted) are scored with a knife so that they bend easily. The outlines (solid lines) are pre-cut, and the net is then ready for folding.

A net ready for folding

Joining

Nets are joined together by tabs (flaps). Nets must always have tabs so they can fit together. The tabs overlap the edges where the sides meet and are glued in place. This is a common way of joining food packaging. Sometimes packages lock together without glue. This is done to reduce the cost of packaging and to increase the speed of production.

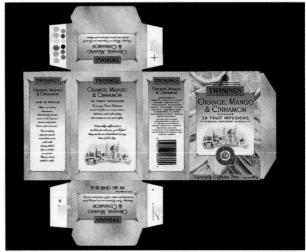

The tabs clip into a slit which is shorter than the overall length of the tabs, locking the sides of the packaging together

Windows

Often designers want to cut a window or opening into the package, so that the customer can see the product. This is true for products like squash balls.

In the photo below, the window is cut across the corner fold so that the ball can be seen from two sides.

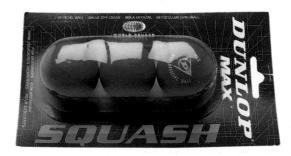

The drawing opposite shows the net for a birdseed box. The container is triangular and has a clear window in the front so the seed can be viewed by the customer.

Folding a package

When folding a package, the fold lines are scored (cut halfway through) with a sharp knife. The main body of the package is formed first, then the edges are glued or slotted into place.

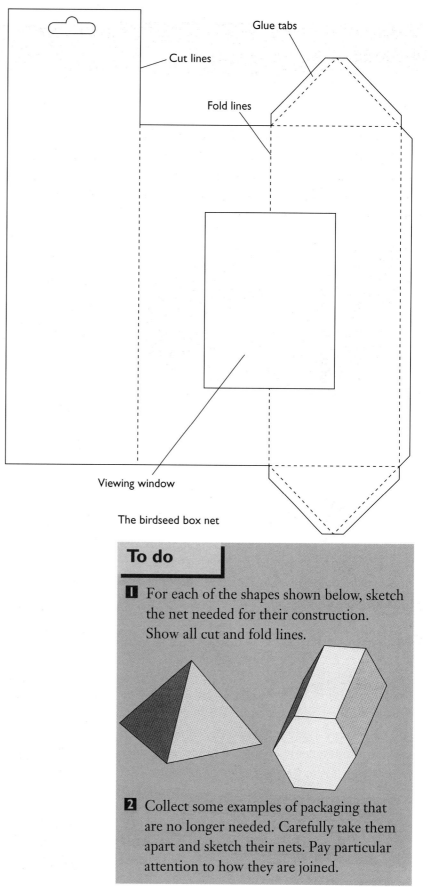

Cut lines

Glue tabs

Fold lines

Viewing window

The birdseed box net

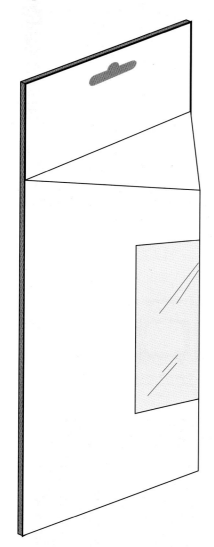

The folded net of the birdseed box

To do

1 For each of the shapes shown below, sketch the net needed for their construction. Show all cut and fold lines.

2 Collect some examples of packaging that are no longer needed. Carefully take them apart and sketch their nets. Pay particular attention to how they are joined.

Information graphics

Getting informed

A range of different sources of information

Information is all around us. We watch television, listen to the radio, use the Internet, read a paper, follow directions, open a packet of cereal and so on. Following instructions and being informed about things is vital to our everyday lives.

Designers of graphic products must develop the skills to visually communicate. Being able to make information and instructions easy to understand and follow, and to create designs that make an impact, are the basis of good design.

Making an impact

Graphic designs that grab your attention by using designs, words or symbols to get a message across are often called 'impact graphics'. Impact graphics use visual persuasion to get people to make choices. Sometimes the choice is to buy a product, other times it is to warn, instruct or inform.

Buy one get one free

An example of an impact graphic

Signs and symbols

One of the simplest and most effective forms of information graphics is the **pictogram.** Pictograms represent words, events or activities. They are simple, easy to understand and, above all, communicate information.

Pictograms designed for the 1972 Olympic Games in Munich are used all over the world

Pictograms do not rely upon language. To be successful they must give messages to people of different nationalities. Pictograms are widely used everywhere. Look at the example below taken from a travel brochure. Ask yourself:

- why the pictograms are used
- what makes a successful pictogram
- why they are black and white.

Holiday brochure pictograms

Signs

When a symbol is used on its own or with other symbols to direct and instruct, it becomes a sign. All of us are used to reading the shorthand of signs. Most people are so familiar with road traffic signs, for example, that they read them, understand them and act upon them without really thinking. These signs, however, are the result of careful design. Symbols and signs are used on a wide variety of graphic products. They are easy to understand and remember.

Examples of road signs

Communicating a process

Symbols are also widely used to explain processes. They help to make a process easier to understand. Look at the process shown on the side of a packet of washing powder. Try and work out what the process is.

DOSAGE INSTRUCTIONS FOR AUTOMATIC MACHINES			
Soft Water	2	2	3
Medium Water	2	2	3
Hard Water	2	2	3
Handwashing or Soaking : These tablets are not recommended for these functions.			

Washing instructions

Using arrows

The correct name for an arrow is a 'directional symbol'. The use of arrows on a graphic product can express a particular direction and force of movement. You can combine words or pictograms with arrows to show something or to help explain a process or direction to follow.

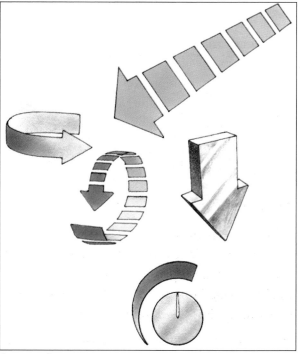

A range of arrow types

To do

1. Make a list of 10 pictograms used around your school. Look at your books, design and technology workshops, the school kitchen and the gym or fitness room. Ask yourself:
   - Are they effective at communicating information?
   - Do they have things in common?
   - How could they be improved?

2. Design a series of pictograms for each of the design and technology rooms. Clearly communicate the different activities that occur within each room.

Logos and trademarks

Logos

Logos (which is short for '**logotypes**') are simple symbols which, like pictograms, are used to convey meaning. Logos tend to be related to a product or organization. Even your school will have a logo. You can find it on your blazer, sweatshirt and headed notepaper. What does your school logo communicate to others? Logos are everywhere. They are part of a graphic language that we have come to understand and accept.

Do you recognize these logos?

Stylization

The word stylization means the process of making a complex graphic into a simple image. Logos must be simple for people to remember them. However, they often convey lots of information about the organization. Sometimes logos that appear very simple on the surface are cleverly designed.

The logo below is for a school called the Kings of Wessex. By using a crown as its logo, the school is drawing upon a common image associated with kings. But when you look closer at the logo, you

will see that the crown is made up of people joining hands, symbolizing a community of people working together.

The main body of the logo is formed around people joining hands

Successful logos

The most successful logos are instantly recognisable. Many people could sketch the Nike logo and the McDonalds golden arches from memory. This is because they are widely used, simple and effective.

Use of colour

Logos often need to be photocopied and used in black and white as well as colour. Because of this, it is important that they are designed with contrasting colours. Contrasting colours make them bold and stand out. A very successful combination is yellow and red. Red is an aggressive colour which stands out and yellow is a light colour that drops into the distance.

The Shell logo uses red and yellow

Trademarks

Trademarks are registered images that can contain a graphic image, company name or slogan. Some companies just use their name on their product as their trademark. Cadbury, Nestlé and Coca Cola are good examples of this. Their trademarks are instantly recognizable even though they do not always use graphic symbols.

What does these products' packaging communicate to the customer?

Trademarks such as this are instantly recognizable

Creating an identity

Logos and trademarks are used by organizations to create a certain identity or image that people will come to know and understand. This image is often referred to as the **corporate identity**. The corporate identity is formed by using the logo or trademark on a range of graphic products. This helps to link all the products in the range together, so that customers can easily identify them.

Image and association

The identity of a product or organization must clearly communicate to the customer what it is about. Products that are designed for cleanliness or hygiene are often white and blue because people associate these colours with cleanliness. White and blue are sterile or cleansing colours and people come to expect them – purple toothpaste is harder to sell than white. Greens and browns are used for 'healthy' products.

The brand name (which is the name of the product) also triggers associations. 'Crunch', 'snaps' and 'chew' are names which are used to

give the customer an idea about the product. A chocolate bar from Cadbury is called *Fuse* because it 'fuses' several different tastes together.

Traditional or modern?

Many companies invent a traditional image for themselves because they believe that customers think that 'if it's traditional it must be good'. Health bars have wrappers with pictures of horse-drawn ploughs and sacks of wheat giving the impression that they are untouched by modern machines, new methods and chemicals. Alternatively, some products deliberately use up-to-date images to create a modern identity. This is important for companies who make products such as computer software, sports and fitness equipment.

To do

1. Sketch three or four common logos. Ask yourself:
   - Which one is the most successful, and why?
   - What do the logos communicate about the company or product?
   - Are they traditional or modern?

2. Design a logo for a shoe company called 'Trax'.

Ergonomics

The 'E' word

Whenever you design anything that is going to be used by humans, you must consider **ergonomics**. Ergonomics is the study of how people work (rest and play) in their environment, which could be an office, school, factory or home. In simple terms ergonomics is about how to make people more efficient at what they do.

Have you ever tried to write with a large, chunky pencil? It feels difficult to hold, it is heavy and, if you use it for a long time, your wrist starts to ache. This is because it is the wrong shape and weight for your hand.

A pencil needs to be easy to grip and comfortable to hold

Take a look at the picture below. The person is sitting at a work desk that has been ergonomically designed.

What has been affected by ergonomics in this picture?

The right environment

So, ergomonics is about making things the right shape, size and weight for humans. But what if the room that you are working in is too hot or too cold? People work best at 'room temperature' which is about 20°C. You cannot work efficiently if you are too hot or too cold. Ergonomics also considers noise, vibration, light and smell. In fact, if any of your senses are uncomfortable you will not work efficiently.

Eg

For someone to work efficiently, the room temperature should be about 20°C

No one can concentrate with too much background noise

For someone to work efficiently, the light should be adequate.

Vibration affects our efficiency at work

No one likes bad smells

Ergonomic graphics

Look at the sign below which is written in an old English style.

A gothic script – this is difficult to read

This style of decorative writing is poorly designed from an ergonomic point of view. It is difficult to read and takes time to work out what it is saying. When designing signs and posters it is important that people can quickly and easily 'get the message'.

Size is important

Can you read this?
Can you read this?
Can you read this?
Can you read this?
Can you read this?
Can you read this?

Look at the pieces of writing above. Which ones are difficult to read?

The size of the text is important. If the writing is too small, people have to strain their eyes to read it.

Style and colour

Some typefaces are easier to read than others. It is important that the one you choose can be easily read. This is particularly true for warning signs where instant communication is essential.

Which style would you choose for the sign below?

DO NOT ENTER DO NOT ENTER

The way colour is used can greatly affect how efficient a graphic product is. Good ergonomic design requires colour contrasts such as red and white.

Nice and clear   **Not so clear**

Colour combinations are important – always try to achieve contrast

Anthropometrics

Anthropometrics is always used with ergonomics. 'Anthropo' means human and 'metrics' means measurement. Anthropometrics is therefore about human measurements. Anthropometric data sheets contain information about the range of human dimensions and sizes for all age groups.

For example, if you measured the nose length of 10,000 18-year-old men, you would find that the graph produced followed a bell-shaped curve.

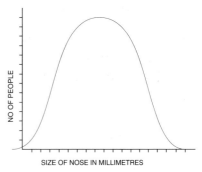

At the left-hand end of the graph are men with small noses. At the right-hand end are men with large noses. The percentages help us to work out how many of the 10,000 men have small, large or average length noses. The vast majority are close to the average. Usually when we design things we try to consider 90 per cent of the population.

Anthropometric data is produced as a series of tables, and these can be found in most libraries.

To do

1. Watch someone preparing a meal in your kitchen at home. See if the kitchen is well designed. Would the meal be prepared quicker if the cooker was moved closer to the sink? Does anything need to be moved to help the cook cut down on time?

2. Look through a magazine and collect examples of good ergonomic graphic design. Cut out the examples and stick them onto an ergonomic poster.

Type and typography

The word type is another word for a letter or character. You will all have heard of the machine called a typewriter which is similar to a computer keyboard and stamps letters onto paper. The art of letter style and design is called **typography**.

Typography is not just about neat lettering or writing. Different letter styles, or typefaces as they are known, can be used to give effect, create meaning or to make an impact. When designing graphic products you need to select typefaces very carefully to achieve the desired outcome.

What does type say?

The typeface chosen can say things about itself. It can express moods or feelings, it can be traditional or modern, exciting or dull.

Times new Roman: **I am traditional**

Nueva: ***I am modern***

ExPonto: *I am artistic*

Helvetica: **I am clear and stand out**

Arial reversed on red: **I shout danger**

Size

Typefaces are measured by the point system. One point (pt) is approximately 0.35mm. A 10pt typeface will therefore be 3.5mm high. The size of the typeface is important. Text that is printed in books is usually no smaller than 10pt because 9pt and below is difficult to read. For headings, a much bigger typeface, such as 16pt, is used. For banner headlines, typefaces as large as 160pt are often used.

10pt Times New Roman	Used for the main text in a book
16pt Heading	A larger point size is used to make a heading stand out – usually 16pt or 18pt
Eg	A 72pt typeface is suitable for making an impact as a headline
P	When designing a poster, sign or display, you will need to use letters that are at least 160pt in size

To ensure that a typeface is easy to read, designers also consider its width and how light or bold it is.

A light typeface needs to be larger to make it easy to read, **but it is easier to read a bold or wide typeface.**

Style

There are literally thousands of different typefaces or fonts to choose from when you design a graphic product. The main styles are:

- serif
- sans serif
- freehand
- stylized.

Serif

Serif typefaces have tails on the ends of the letters.

 Serif typefaces are often used for the main text (body text) in books because they are easy on the eye and 'comfortable' to read

Sans serif

The word 'sans' comes from the French word which means 'without'. Sans serif typefaces do not have tails; they are plain and clear.

 Sans serif typefaces are used for information and warning signs because they are clear and simple

Freehand

Freehand looks like a person's handwriting and seems more personal than other typefaces.

Freehand typefaces are so called because they are often similar in style to a person's own handwriting. They are used because they appear to be personal

Stylized

Stylized typefaces are designed to help communicate meaning. They are often found on products such as chocolate bars.

Examples of stylized typefaces. They show what the product is like

Designing typefaces

Designing new stylized typefaces as titles for your project sheets can help to bring your work to life. As with any designing skill, it takes a good deal of practice. It is a good idea to use squared or grid paper to help you work out the size and width of the letters. Practise with different letter styles until you find a good design. This can then be traced through onto your work.

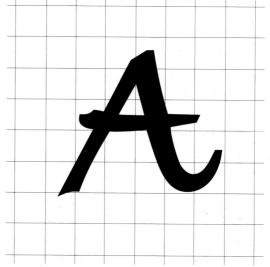

Using grid paper helps you to work out the size and width of the letters. When the design is complete it can be used as a template for your work

To do

1. Collect as many different examples of typefaces as you can and stick them into a design scrapbook. Try to arrange them under headings such as 'serif' and 'stylized'. Find large sizes that you could use as trace-through templates for your own work.

2. Design a stylized typeface for a new chocolate bar which is to be called 'Cruncher'.

Think about how the typeface design will communicate to customers what the product is like. Use colour carefully and design a letter style that reflects the contents and also gives the impression of a 'crunch'.

Grids and layouts

Grids

When graphic designers produce layouts for products such as packaging and posters, their designs are usually based on a grid.

If you take a close look at this book, you will notice that the pages have certain similarities. They use the same size and style of typeface for headings, subheadings and body text. The colours are consistent. The position of the page numbers is the same.

Also you will notice that all the text is fitted into two columns. This is because the book is based upon a grid.

Designers spend a long time thinking about layout and producing ideas and sketches. All newspapers, leaflets and magazines use a grid for their layout. This helps to give the product a visual style, which can be used on every page.

To do

Collect a number of different magazines. Place a large piece of tracing paper over a double page (that is, two facing pages). Using a pencil and ruler, carefully sketch out the grid that has been used to lay out the page.

The same style and size is used for headings

The text is in two columns

The colours are consistent

The same style and size of typeface is used for the subheadings

The position of the page numbers is the same

A page from this book

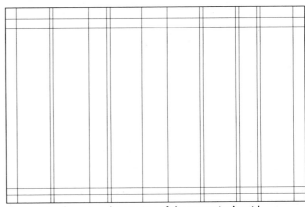

A magazine layout and a tracing of the magazine's grid

Layouts

Grids are useful when designing your own layouts. Grids take quite a long time to prepare but, once they have been produced, they can be slipped under your design sheets and used over and over again.

When designing products of your own, you need to think about how you want your graphic product to look. It is a good idea to make a series of sketches of possible layouts first. These simple sketches will help to give you some idea about how the final design will look.

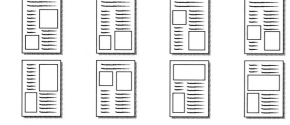

Simple sketches of possible layouts

In your designs should consider:

- the number of columns
- the width of the margins
- the position of the headings
- the position of the pictures
- what colours and combinations of colours are to be used.

Text layout

Text can be arranged in different ways on a page to produce different types of layout. The most common types of text layout are:

- centre justified
- right justified
- left justified
- fully justified.

The word justified, or 'justification' as it is sometimes used, means **alignment**. So, 'right justified' means that the text is aligned to the right, and so on.

Centre justification

This is used when each line of the text needs to be centred on the page or column. It is often used on fold-out leaflets and posters but is rarely used in books.

Left justification

This means that the text is aligned to the left. It is used to line up the text next to a margin on the edge of a page or sometimes next to an illustration in the middle of a page.

Right justification

This is the opposite to left justified. It aligns the text to the right side. It is often used to align text next to a picture or photograph.

Fully justified

This is when the text is aligned on both the right-hand and left-hand margin. It is often used for columns in newspapers and magazines. Because words vary in length, the spaces between the letters have to be adjusted in order to make the text 'look right'.

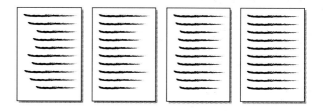

Text arranged as (from left to right) right justified, left justified, centre justified and fully justified

To do

Imagine you have been asked to design a series of posters on music and popular bands. The posters must all use the same basic layout and contain headlines, pictures of the band and information for the fans.

Design a grid that could be used as the basic layout for each of the posters. The grid should be based upon an A4 sheet and should give all the necessary details for the poster's design.

Grids as underlays

As we have already discovered, graphic designers usually base their layout designs on grids. Grids are particularly useful when used as **underlays.** An underlay slips underneath the page you are working on and allows you to trace through. The simplest type of underlay is a line guide. The line guide helps the desginer to keep all written text horizontal without having to draw pencil guidelines on the page.

A line guide helps you to keep your writing straight without having to draw guidelines

Column guides

Column guides are similar to line guides except that they separate the page into two, three or four columns. Column guides are particularly useful when presenting research or product analysis sheets. They enable you to cut and stick pictures and diagrams onto the page and keep the writing in a column.

Column guides are similar to the layouts used in a book.

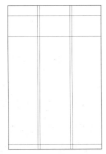

Examples of a column guide

Drawing with grids

When you need to produce accurate sketches quickly, there are a number of different grids that you can use.

Squared grid

Squared grids are most useful for producing orthographic sketches. With a squared grid, the front elevation (view), end elevation and plan are easy to place by following the lines on the grid.

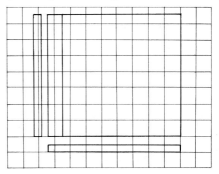

An orthographic drawing of a CD box

Isometric grid

Isometric grids consist of lines at 30 degrees from the horizontal, together with vertical lines. Isometric grids are difficult to make yourself, but you can buy them. Drawing isometric sketches with a grid is simple and quick.

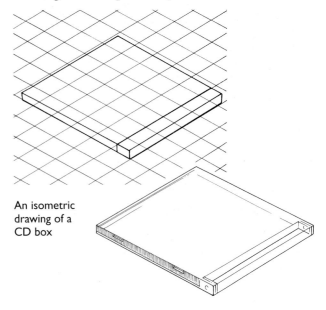

An isometric drawing of a CD box

Perspective grids

Perspective grids can be either one or two point perspective (see pages 34–5). With a perspective grid, the object can be drawn either vertically or on its side, depending on which way up you have the grid.

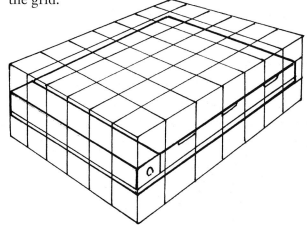

A CD box is drawn on this perspective grid

Probably the most common perspective grid is the single point perspective grid used by kitchen designers and interior designers. It shows three walls of a room. By using this grid, the designer is able to draw all the units and equipment needed for a new kitchen or other room.

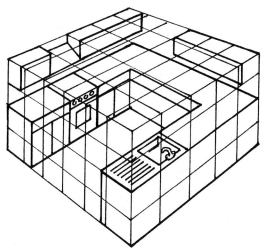

A simple kitchen design is drawn on this perspective grid

These days, most kitchen design is carried out on the computer using **computer-aided design** (CAD) software. This software uses a grid in the same way as you would if you were producing it by hand.

Fashion design

In the same way that layout grids are used by graphic designers for producing sketches, people underlays are used to quickly sketch fashion ideas. These underlays can be quick and easy to produce, by tracing through from photographs of fashion models found in magazines. They improve the presentation of your ideas because they enable you to draw your ideas directly onto the models themselves.

People underlays are produced by tracing photographs of fashion models

To do

Produce a series of text underlays for your design and technology projects. Choose a suitable typeface that can be used throughout your work.

A range of graphic products

The finished product

The final stage in the production of graphic products takes place at the printers. It is here that designs are produced in the form that they will appear in shops.

There are many ways of printing and each technique has its own advantages and disadvantages.

Two-colour printing

The most simple technique involves producing a **plate** which is coated with ink and pressed against the surface to be printed. This is similar to potato printing or stamping. Machines that use this basic process are called **letterpress** printers. Although it is called two-colour printing it is really only one colour because the paper provides the second colour. Letterpress printing is a cheap process that is used for printing business cards, leaflets and letterheads in small numbers.

Printing with four colours

If you take packaging such as a cereal packet apart, you will find on one of the glue tabs four spots that are coloured blue, yellow, red and black. These colour marks show the four colours that are used for printing. They are basically the three primary colours plus black.

These colours are called **process colours**. Their correct names are cyan (blue), magenta (red), yellow and K (black), known as CMYK for short. By mixing the four process colours together, all the other colours can be achieved. (See colour theory, pages 48 and 49.)

Types of four-colour printing

Lithography

This process is widely used for producing leaflets, books and point of sale displays. It can produce high quality print and is relatively cheap. The process involves making a printing plate (usually from aluminium) which has the image etched onto it. The printing plate is washed with a special chemical that makes the etched area attractive to the ink. The non-print areas repel the ink.

Because of the cost of making the printing plate, lithography is an expensive process if only a few hundred copies are required. Lithography is best for over 1000 copies in single or multiple colours.

A lithography print machine

Screen printing

Sometimes the object to be printed is an awkward shape, or made from a textile material. One simple way of printing these objects is to use **screen printing.** Screen printing is not like other ways of printing, and uses a stencil, through which the ink is pushed. It is called screen printing because the ink is forced through a very fine mesh (called a screen) which helps to spread it evenly across the stencil.

The stencil is made from card, or sometimes paper. Screen printing is simple to do but is quite time-consuming. It is a relatively cheap process if only a small quantity of printed items is required. It is an ideal process for simple designs, such as signs and displays. High quality printouts can be achieved by using special photographic stencils.

The screen printing process

Examples of screen-printed products

Questions

Using reference books or the Internet, find out about the history of printing. Answer the following questions:

1 Who invented the first printing press?

2 What is block printing?

Posters and merchandizing

Selling with graphics

Posters are widely used to generate interest in a product or event. As with all materials that are designed to promote, they must attract people's attention, and create interest and desire.

Posters form the basis of advertizing campaigns because they are cheap to produce and can be easily displayed in shop windows and on billboards. Posters always contain a mixture of graphics and information.

Posters

Posters usually use photographs or images to attract attention. When an event such as a film or video is being advertized, characters from the film are nearly always shown. This helps people to immediately recognize and understand what the poster is about.

An exciting part from the play or film is often shown. Sometimes the photograph is taken directly from the film and at other times it is put together by the graphic designer. When promoting a product such as a film, the title of the film and names of actors and performers are included, together with with other important information, to help make the image effective.

A poster to advertise the film *The World is not Enough*

To do

1. Look carefully at the poster above and answer the following questions:

   a How does the poster create impact?

   b What does it tell you about the film?

   c What are the main colours used for the text, and why?

Merchandizing

When a new product such as a television programme or film becomes popular, manufacturers often use this success to increase the sales of their own products. This is known as **merchandizing**. Merchandizing is good for both companies because it gives free publicity to the film or programme and helps to increase sales of the product.

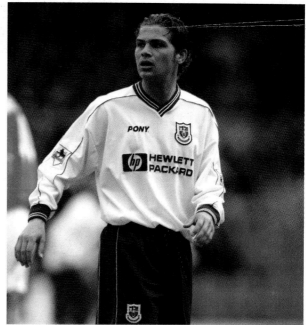

A footballer has his sponsor's name on his shirt

A range of merchandizing products

Merchandizing is part of **product promotion.** Promoting a product involves developing ways of making it more popular and increasing its sales. Large companies invest huge sums of money in sponsorship. Football teams have company names on their shirts and players are paid for wearing a particular type of boot.

Most pop bands promote their new CDs or singles by a music tour. They use merchandizing, such as T-shirts with their picture on, to help promote their tour. People who go to the concerts want a souvenir and this in turn provides free advertizing for the band.

Printed T-shirts help to promote a band

To do

1. Think of as many examples of posters and merchandizing packaging as you can. Make a list of the different kinds of product and free gifts that use the image to help sell the product.

2. Design a poster to promote your favourite film.

Unwrapping the pack

Made to be thrown away

It is said that about 80 per cent of all household rubbish comes from packaging. We buy products, unwrap the pack and then throw away the packaging – what a waste!

A range of packaging

What is the point of packaging?

To answer this question we have to look at the three functions of packaging. These are to sell, protect and communicate.

Selling the product

For packaging, as for all graphic products, the impact of the design is very important. People often make decisions based on first impressions, sometimes without even thinking about it. Some of the most successful brands in the world use a bright red background. This is because red stands out, especially when a contrasting colour like white is used for the product name. Gold is seen as a mark of quality. Athletes are awarded a gold medal when they win a race as proof that they are the best. Gold is used in this way with products. They are saying 'buy me, I am the best'. It is the packaging that helps to sell the product to the customer.

Protecting the product

The clever design of an egg box provides excellent protection for its fragile product

Probably the most important function of packaging is to protect a product from breaking, soiling or, in the case of foods, perishing. What good would a tin of baked beans be without the tin? How many eggs would get broken in a supermarket trolley if they weren't in a box?

Food must be protected, by law. Most foods need to be sealed to prevent them from exposure to the atmosphere. The packaging has to be there for protection, so why not also use it to help sell the product?

Other products, such as screws and nails, are held in blister packaging so that they are kept together and not lost.

Cheese is packaged in vacuum-sealed, clear plastic which allows the customer to see the product. Being able to see the product is important to many customers

Communicating the product

Packaging communicates two different types of information: the written and the unwritten.

The written

By law, packaging must display certain information, such as the type of product, its weight and details of the company that made it. It will often give the buyer instructions on how to use the product. In the case of food, these instructions will usually be about cooking and freezing. There is also a barcode which gives coded information to the shopkeeper. Information like this is usually kept on the back of the packaging because it does not help to sell the product.

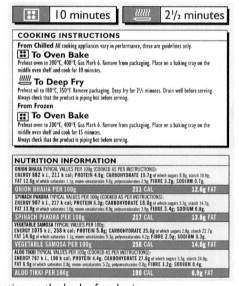

Information on the back of packaging

The unwritten

Unwritten information is less obvious and often you have to analyse the packaging to work out what is being communicated. Cat food tins always show pictures of well fed, happy looking cats; chocolate boxes don't tell you that their contents are full of sugar. The design of packaging also helps to target the product at the right market. Compare the differences between a packet of white chocolate sweets with a pot of low calorie yoghurt. Products designed for children tend to use bright, vivid colours and child-friendly images. Products designed for

adults tend to use more sedate colours like grey and are often quite plain. The design communicates clearly who the product is for.

Making use of packaging

Many products have 'street credibility' as brands. The product packaging is often highly regarded. One way of extending the life of the packaging, and preventing it from being thrown away, is to make something useful out of it.

The Paper Clock Company project

The Paper Clock Company is a company that converts highly regarded packaging into clocks. Your task is to design and make a packaging paper clock.

Example of a clock made from discarded perfume packaging

To do

Collect three or four examples of product packaging that is designed for different types of people, such as children, men, women and teenagers.

Look carefully at the packaging and compare the differences between each of the packages. In particular, think carefully about how they sell, protect and communicate their products. Pay particular attention to the use of colour, pictures, images and text.

Materials for packaging

Choosing the right material

There is wide range of materials that you can use for producing your packaging designs. Each material has its advantages and disadvantages. Whenever you design a graphic product you must decide what properties the material needs to have and write these in the design specification. Some are rigid, some flexible. Some are waterproof and some are not.

What different sorts of packaging have been used here?

Paper and board

Papers come in a variety of colours, weights and textures. The choice of paper is important and can greatly affect the quality of the final product. Paper is weighed in grams (gm) per square metre. A 90gm paper means that one piece measuring 1 metre x 1 metre will weigh 90gm.

Paper sizes

The most common range of paper sizes is the 'A' range. You will be most familiar with A4 paper. Each time the paper is halved in size, its value goes up by one. So, A4 is half the size of A3, A3 is half the size of A2, and so on.

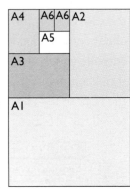

A paper size chart

Boards

Boards basically are heavy paper. Usually papers become boards when their weight is greater than 200 gm per square metre. Some are duplex (two pieces joined together) and have two different coloured surfaces. Boards can be made very strong and light by having a corrugated inside. Sometimes boards have an aluminum foil coating to make them waterproof.

Material	Advantages	Used for
Newsprint	Lightweight, accepts all types of ink	Newspapers
Cartridge paper	Good quality, provides a good surface for pencil, pens, markers	Design drawings, sketch pads
Sugar paper	Has contrasting colours which are useful for tonal drawings	Mounting work, displays
Cardboard	Cheap, rigid, good printing surface, recyclable	Packaging, cartons and boxes
Corrugated card	Very strong, lightweight, recyclable	Packaging fragile products
White board	Bleached surface, very strong, excellent for printing	Book covers, quality packaging
Duplex board	Cheaper than solid white board, provides an alternative textured surface for printing	Food packaging

Different types of paper used for graphic products

Plastic

Plastics are widely used in packaging because they are cheap, tough, easily printed onto and are usually 'squeezee' which makes them perfect for bottles.

Bottles and containers

These are often made by a process of blow moulding. A thin tube of hot plastic is gripped between the two halves of a bottle-shaped mould and air is blown in. The tube then takes the shape of the mould and the bottle is formed.

A variety of plastic containers

Blister packaging

Another common use of plastics in packaging is blister packaging. A thin plastic film is heated up and **vacuum formed** over the product, protecting it and sealing it from air. It also helps to keep the product securely in place.

Blister packaging is widely used for protecting and containing products

Common plastics	Used for
Polyvinyl chloride (PVC)	Quite brittle – used for blister packs
Polystyrene (expanded)	Used for protection (and filling bean bags)
Polypropylene	Tough and rigid – used for toothbrushes
Polythene (low density)	Carrier bags
Polythene (high density)	Drinks containers

Different types of plastics and their uses

Glass

Glass is still widely used in packaging, particularly for food products that are preserved, like jam. It has the advantage of being see-through and, because it is quite heavy, it gives the impression of good quality. It does not flavour the product at all and can be easily recycled. Unlike most plastics, it easily breaks and is therefore relatively dangerous.

Glass is commonly used for drinks containers

Metals

The most common metals in packaging are steel and aluminium. Aluminium is very light and does not rust. It is easy to form and can be printed on. It is recyclable. Steel is cheaper yet heavier than aluminium and must be plated with a non-rusting metal before it can be used. It is most widely used for tins in food packaging. It can be recycled.

Aluminium is the most common metal used for soft drinks cans although steel can also be used

Research

Find as much information as you can about paper making. Trace back through history and find out which nation 'discovered' paper. Find out about the materials used to make paper and how they affect its texture and quality.

Using machines and equipment

There is wide variety of processes that you can use to produce your packaging designs. Some use machines to help you form the designs and others use craft techniques.

Vacuum forming

This is a cheap and useful way of producing simple forms in thin plastic sheet. It is used for producing blister packaging and shapes for containing and displaying products, such as clear Easter egg trays.

Vacuum-formed Easter egg trays

Making a vacuum form mould (for an Easter egg)

A material, usually wood, is carefully formed into the exact shape of half the egg. When making a mould it is important that there are clear angles on all sides so that the plastic will easily come off the mould when it has been formed. Tiny holes are drilled around the base and over the surface of the mould, so that when the air is removed by the vacuum pump, the plastic film will wrap around it completely and no air will be trapped.

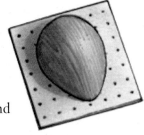

A vacuum form mould for an Easter egg

The process of vacuum forming

The vacuum forming machine consists of a heating element for heating the plastic, a platform that can be raised and lowered, and a vacuum pump.

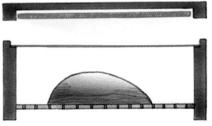

1 The mould is placed in the vacuum forming machine and a thin sheet of plastic is secured above it.

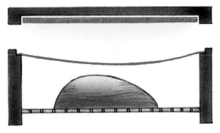

2 The plastic is heated until it becomes very floppy.

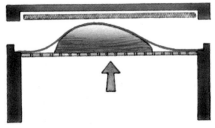

3 The vacuum pump is turned on. This sucks out all the air between the plastic and the mould.

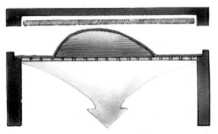

4 The plastic is sucked down over the mould. When the plastic is cool it sets into the shape of the mould.

Laminating

Plastic laminating is a process used to protect graphic products from moisture. Laminating machines use heat and pressure to sandwich the work between two layers of plastic film.

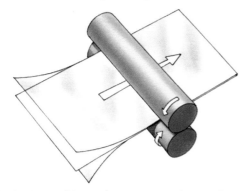

Laminating is a useful way of protecting products such as menus

Blow moulding

Blow moulding is commonly used to make bottles and containers. It is based on the process of glass blowing that has been used for thousands of years. In plastic blow moulding, a thin tube of hot plastic is gripped tightly between two halves of a bottle-shaped mould. Hot air is then blown under pressure into the tube. The air forces the tube outwards so that it takes the shape of the mould.

Blow moulding machines are expensive to buy, although the process is quick and easy. Blow moulding will only produce simple shapes, although handles and screw threads can be formed.

Using the blow moulding process, a plastic bottle can be produced

Special effects

One way of producing interesting backgrounds and effects on paper and card is to use the process of marbling. Marbling is based on the principle that oil and water do not mix. A small quantity of oil-based paints is spread out on the surface of water in a tank and then mixed with a stick. Dipping the paper or card into the tank will transfer the paint pattern onto the paper.

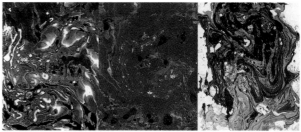

Examples of marbelling

Often when we use plain manufactured woods that have no grain, like medium density fibreboard (MDF), it is difficult to get them to look attractive. Marbling can be used to rectify this although a background colour must first be used.

Example of marbling on MDF

To do

Using either soft clay or papier mâché, design and produce a mask that could be worn to a fancy dress party. When completed, the mask can be used as a mould for vacuum forming.

CHECK the size of your school's vacuum forming machine before you start.

Using ICT

What is ICT?

ICT stands for information and communications technology and it relates to how computers can help to make us better informed and to work more efficiently. ICT is not just about the **Internet,** it is about a whole range of different ways of communicating. Using ICT could help you improve the quality and accuracy of your work.

ICT in design and technology

Take a look at the design process below. For most stages of the process there are suggestions for how ICT could improve the quality of your design work.

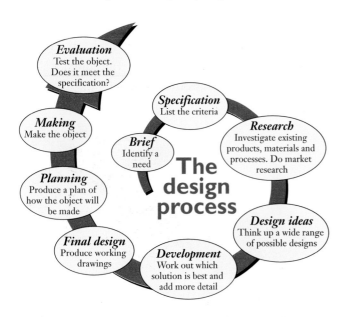

Design ideas

Use a digital camera and photo-editing software to change existing pictures. Use computer-aided design (CAD) software to create graphic ideas quickly and easily. These can be rotated and modified.

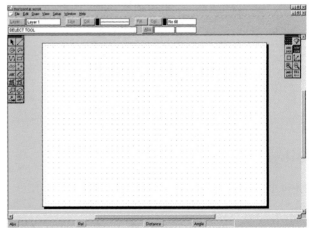

A CAD design screen

Development

Use a database or CD-ROM to find out about the most appropriate materials for your design. Use computer-aided manufacture (CAM) software to make a model of your solution.

	A	B	C	D	E
1	Graphic Product	Material	size	Quantity	Method of printing
2	Display	White card	A3	1	Lithography
3	Business card	White card	B6	2000	Letterpress
4	Flyer	90gm paper	A4	5000	Lithography
5	Poster	150gm paper	A2	1000	Lithography
6	Credit card	Thin plastic	B6	300	Thermo formed
7	Video insert	90gm paper	A5	1000	Lithography
8	CD insert	90gm paper	B5	1000	Lithography

A database screen showing suitable materials for different designs

To do

Surf the Internet to find information about your product. Access websites directly. E-mail companies and ask for information about their products. Visit virtual factories on the Internet to see how manufacturing is carried out in industry.

Final design

Use a 3-D scanner to scan the design from your high quality prototype model. Use graphics or publishing software to produce publicity materials to advertize your product.

Example of an advert for your product

Planning

Use a spreadsheet to work out detailed costings for your product.

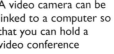

Example of a costing spreadsheet

Making

Computer-aided manufacture can be used to make the final product, such as a computer-controlled plotter/cutter.

Computer-controlled vinyl cutter for making signs

Evaluation

A video conference means that you can show your ideas to your client, or a person in industry using a video camera that is linked to a computer. Use a word processing package to write a detailed report about your product. Use a scanner to illustrate modifications.

A video camera can be linked to a computer so that you can hold a video conference

To do

1. Find out about the range of information technology facilities at your school. Suggest ways that each program or piece of equipment could be used for graphics work.

2. Describe ways you could use the Internet to find information for your food technology research.

Scanners and digital cameras

Scanners

In recent years graphic designers have come to rely more and more on scanners in the design of graphic products. A scanner is a device that creates an electronic map of a picture. This map is made up of a series of dots or **pixels.** The quality of the picture is determined by how many pixels there are per square millimetre. This is called the **resolution**.

A scanner produces an electronic map of the image made up of a series of dots or pixels

Hint

High resolution images require a large amount of computer memory, especially on colour pictures. Use a black and white image or low resolution if you can.

Using scanners

Scanners are particularly useful in design and technology projects because they allow you to add photographs and realistic pictures to your work. This helps you to make high quality products that look like the real thing.

Digital cameras

A digital camera

Digital cameras are a cross between a normal camera and a scanner. You use them just like a normal camera but instead of the images being captured on photographic film, they are saved on a computer disc.

Digital cameras have a small screen at the back of the camera that allows you to see the picture once you have taken it. This means that if you are not happy with it you can delete it and start again.

Getting the pictures onto the computer

Once the pictures have been taken, they need to be transferred to a computer. The camera is connected to the computer with a cable, and special computer software is used to transfer the images. This is called uploading. Once the images have been uploaded to the computer, they are saved as files that can be opened and closed in the normal way. This allows you to use them either directly as they are or load them into design software and modify them to suit.

Digital editing

When pictures have been scanned or uploaded to the computer they are saved as **digital** images. These pictures or images can now be changed or **edited** using photo-editing software. The most common forms of editing are 'cropping' which means cutting a picture down to size, 'rotating' or 'resizing' it. In addition, the individual pixels can have their colour changed, be deleted or deformed in some way. Doing this will help you to create interesting graphic products.

A picture showing how photographs can be edited using photo-editing software

A design project

'Use photo-editing software to produce a set of stamps for a country'

This design project was given to a group of students on a graphic products course. The original pictures were downloaded from one of the photo gallery websites on the Internet. Alternatively, pictures could have been scanned from a book or uploaded from a digital camera.

The first task was to load a stamp background from a **clip art** library.

Then a country had to be chosen and a suitable set of pictures acquired. For this stamp, a picture from Florence, Italy was used and added to the background of the stamp.

The photograph is added to the stamp outline

The final task was to add the text. At this stage, research was carried out into the language, the currency and other necessary details.

A completed set of stamps, with text added, using the theme of Italy. On these stamps images from other pictures have been cut out and pasted onto the original photographs.

To do

Scan a photograph of yourself and use photo-editing software to produce a membership card to the Design and Technology Club.

Computer-aided design

The computer is just a tool

Many people think that somehow computers will replace designers. This is not the case. They can, however, make the work of a designer much quicker and easier. As the name suggests, computer-aided design (**CAD**) is a computer software program that assists designers in their work.

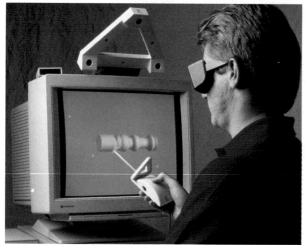

A CAD program being used by a designer

Features of CAD programs

Most computer-aided design software requires you to produce orthographic (2-D) drawings. These programs have a library of the correct symbols, and will automatically add dimensions to your work as you draw. As with any other drawing package, CAD software lets you fill areas with colour or with hatched lines.

A motor bike produced using a computer-aided design package. Filling and hatching help to make the drawing clearer

Speeding things up and getting it right

In hand-drawing, whenever we make a mistake we have to rub it out and start again. Sometimes we need to alter a drawing half way through. All these things are time-consuming and frustrating to the designer. With CAD, making changes such as resizing is easy to do. Being able to rotate or duplicate an object are other useful features.

Computer-aided design is widely used in industry. Using CAD, designers can see a model of an object. This means that a product can be seen from all angles, simply by rotating the image. A car designer, for example, can open and close doors on a car, change colours and wheel types all at a touch of the mouse.

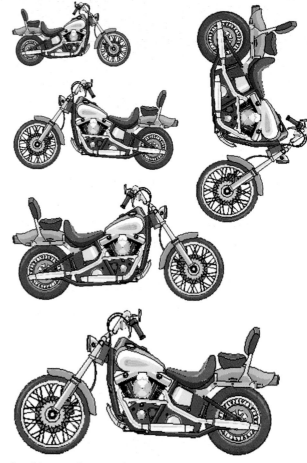

An object can be resized or rotated easily and quickly

Computer-aided design in action

Computers are widely used to model components and products on the screen. This means that designs can be **evaluated** before they are made.

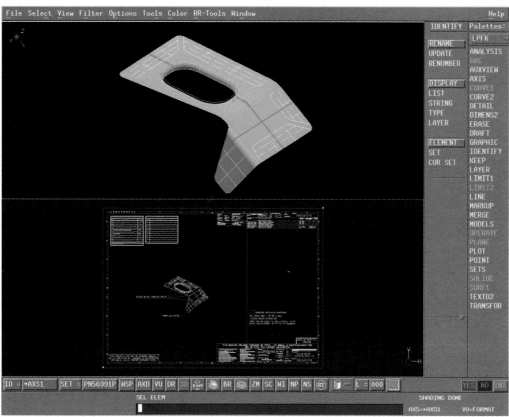

This CAD screen shows an early design drawing for a car body

Working drawings

In your design and technology projects, the most useful way of using CAD is to help you produce working drawings. A working drawing gives dimensions and all the details needed to make your designs.

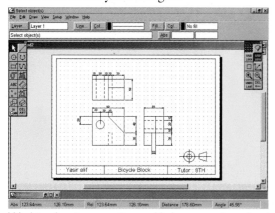

Working drawings save time and help you produce drawings that are accurate

Hint

Look for opportunities to use CAD to help you prepare your drawings. It will save you time and improve the quality of your work.

Questions

1. List three objects you think have been designed with the use of CAD.

2. Explain the advantages and disadvantages of using CAD when designing.

Computer-aided manufacture

In control

Computers help designers to design products and have the advantage of being quicker and more accurate than humans. The same is true for making products. Computers are fitted into machines to control their movements. The computer is given a set of instructions in the form of a computer program that tells it exactly what to do. Unlike humans, computers do not need a break, they don't go on holiday and they can work 24 hours a day, seven days a week.

In industry, more and more manufacturing processes are controlled by computers. Robots can do dangerous tasks which would be unsafe for humans. With the help of computer-aided manufacturing (CAM) production is now very fast. Large motor manufacturers, such as Volkswagen, can produce a complete car in less than 24 hours.

The use of CAM in production

CAM and graphic products

Computer-aided manufacture is widely used for the manufacture of graphic products. The starting point for this process is the final design or the working drawing. The device that is going to make the product is connected to the computer by a cable and is set up with the correct materials. The CAM machine is able to understand the commands from the computer and follows the instructions.

Making signs

Very thin plastic (vinyl) can be accurately cut out and used to make signs by a CAM cutter. The sign is first designed using a CAD program. The size of the sign must be accurately worked out before cutting. When the sign has been cut, the waste is 'picked out' and the vinyl is transferred to the plastic base using special adhesive film.

A pupil using a scanner/cutter

The waste is 'picked out' from the cut sign

Some CAM machines use a rotating cutter rather than a static knife. These are called router or milling machines. Large CAM milling machines are widely used in industry, but they are expensive. Small CAM machines can be useful for graphic products projects as engraving tools. Designs can be cut out of solid plastic and used as plaques or logos on bigger products.

An example of a student's work using CAM. The logo is machined onto clear acrylic that has been painted black

Scanner/cutters

Many CAM machines used in school do not need to be linked to computers. They have a scanner which can make an exact copy of a product.

Below is a scanner/cutter. The design is fed into the machine and a copy is cut directly onto the vinyl.

A scanner/cutter

Below is a three-dimensional scanner/cutter. A full body scan of the object is made and a model is then cut out. The model can be bigger or smaller. This is particularly useful for making components for models that have to be very accurate.

A three-dimensional scanner/cutter

Embroidery

Graphic product design often involves designing logos for companies and organizations. One way that these designs are used is on uniforms. A good way of producing these logos on clothes is to use computer-controlled sewing machines.

These sewing machines are able to work from scanned images of designs. The machine is set up with the right colour cotton and the design is produced.

To do

Write a list of the advantages and disadvantages of using computer-aided manufacture to make products. Can you think of a situation where CAM would never be used?

Cyber graphics

The world at your fingertips

A whole new language has developed over the last few years since the dawn of the Internet. Words like **cyberspace**, **e-mail** and **search engine** are now part of our everyday vocabulary. The Internet (sometimes referred to as the 'information super highway') is a network of interconnected computers around the world. This world where people are linked together electronically is referred to as cyberspace.

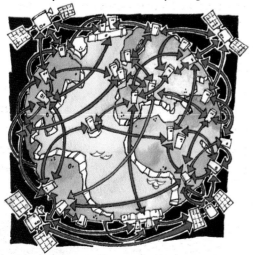

Computers, telephone wires and satellites link people from around the world

Using the Internet

All you need to plug into cyberspace is a computer, a **modem** and a telephone line. A modem is an electronic device that converts the digital signals from the computer into sound signals that can be sent down the telephone line. A modem works in reverse when it receives signals from other people.

Because it is relatively easy to publish materials on the Internet, there is an astonishing range of information that can be found. This can be invaluable to you when you need to carry out research for your design and technology projects.

Looking at websites

Each company or individual who sets up an information page on the Internet has an address. In the same way that you can find where someone lives by using their postal address, searching for a particular Internet address will lead you to a website.

For example, if you typed in *http://www.cadbury.co.uk* you would be taken to the website for Cadbury. This website is divided into sections to help you find your way around (navigate). It contains links to information about chocolate production, manufacturing and marketing, as well as pictures, and a wide range of other information.

The design of websites like these must be clear and simple. Just like a book, websites must have an index, clear headings and simple-to-follow instructions. They must also be interesting and informative. The best websites make you feel as though you are virtually there!

link   link   The Cadbury website

Designing a webpage

In the same way that graphic designers have traditionally designed leaflets, brochures, advertizing campaigns etc, they are now called upon to design webpages. Webpage design is different from designing a book or leaflet. Pages do not have to fit into a particular grid or size, they can be as long or short as necessary and there is no limit on the number of pictures or images used.

When designing a website it is important to remember that everyone will see the site slightly differently. This is because the quality of computer monitors can vary enormously. Therefore, unlike a book which is the same for all readers, small complex images and text may not work.

Unlike a book which is published then rarely changed, a webpage must be constantly updated. Design is only the start.

Design in action

Peter is a young design and technology student who is particularly interested in cyber graphics.

Peter is currently studying A level design and technology, and is particularly interested in graphic products

As a life-long football fan and keen supporter of Bolton Wanderers, Peter was asked to design the official Bolton Wanderers Supporters Association webpage. The webpage needed to have information about the club and its players, and details about matches that they had played.

Making it instantly recognizable

Peter had to make the webpage instantly recognizable and ensure the connection with football was obvious. The use of the Bolton Wanderers logo and a spinning football helps people to instantly recognize the site.

An image from the Bolton Wanderers Supporters Association website

Clear layout

Reading text on a computer screen can be quite difficult. The choice of text, its size and colour are important to the design. Peter decided to design the website using a conventional layout, simple yet bold images, and good colour contrast.

The Bolton Wanderers Supporters Association website (http://www.bwsa.cwc.net)

To do

Use the Internet to look for design and technology webpages. Look carefully at the design of two or three of them. Make a list of the good features of each site and why you like them.

What is a model?

There are basically two types of model: a mock-up which is made during the design development stage, and a product model which can be the outcome of a design project.

Why make a model?

Models are useful to the designer because they help to give a better understanding of what the final product may look like. It is difficult to decide on whether a design is acceptable or not just by looking at a drawing. A full-scale model allows the designer to carry out tests and evaluations without having to go through the expense of making the real thing.

Motor manufacturers make a full-scale model in clay in to evaluate the appearance and function of a new car design

How to model

Graphic designers use whatever materials they have available to make models. From wood, metal and plastic through to buttons and even sweets – virtually anything can be used to make models look realistic. If a model is just a mock-up or a simple test, the level of detail needed is not as high as a final product model, which should be as close to the real thing as possible.

Scale

For a model to be useful for testing, it must be made to a scale. If existing figures of people are to be used with the model, this will determine its scale. It is best to choose a scale which is easy to work out, such as 1:2, 1:5 or 1:10. For example, 1:2 means that 1mm on the model equals 2mm on the actual product, 1:5 means that 1mm on the model equals 5mm on the product and so on. If you are making an architectural model of a large building you will need to use a much smaller scale, such as 1:250.

Using actual figures of people, such as this action man, will determine the scale of your model

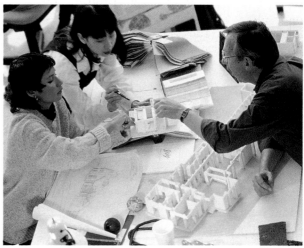

Architectural models are made to a small scale

The computer

Computer models are a quick and inexpensive way of looking at the three-dimensional form of a product. The image of a product can be created on a computer monitor and realistic colour and shading applied. Sophisticated computer programs allow this image to be rotated so that it can be seen from different angles.

Test Models

Sometimes, when we are designing a product that has to work or function in a particular way, it is necessary to make a test model. Test models do not necessarily have to look like the real thing as long as the working part of the model is realistic.

This map shows one method of folding

Products that have a mechanism, for example a lever, crank or pulley, can be tested using construction kits such as Lego. In this way the designer can tell if the basic idea will work or function before further developing the design.

Construction kits such as Lego are useful for testing to see if working parts of a model function according to plan

Presentation models

One of the main uses of a model is for the designer to show clients how the idea will look in real life. The model is used, along with high quality rendered drawings, in a product presentation. The finished model will be made to look exactly like the real product. Designers usually employ professional model makers to make these models.

Presentation models in action

When designing a product such as an electrical appliance, designs that look good on paper can only be fully evaluated by looking at a presentation model. In this example, a design and technology student has used medium density fibreboard (MDF) to make a presentation model of his design for a new coffee machine.

The finished model of a coffee machine

To do

Look carefully at toy models of humans. Measure their proportions, and:

  a work out their scale

  b decide if they are an accurate representation of the human form.

Modelling

Modelling materials

In schools the most common materials used for modelling are MDF, cardboard and thin plastic. In addition fillers, paints, plaster of Paris and anything else you can lay your hands on can be used.

Medium density fibreboard (MDF)

MDF is made from wood dust that is pressed together, glued and formed into large boards.

MDF is widely used for making small product models. Because it is a manufactured board and not a natural timber, it does not have any grain. This means that it does not split easily and can be formed into quite intricate shapes.

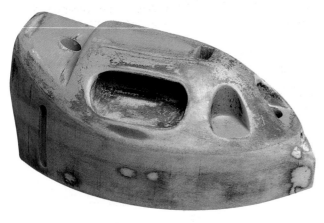

A model of an iron made from MDF

Hint

Because MDF is made from fine dust and glue, care must be taken. An extractor must be used when it is being machined.

Expanded foam

Expanded foams, such as polystyrene, are used by designers to make concept models. A concept model does not have any detail but helps to give an impression of the shape, form and size of a product. Expanded foams are crumbly and do not allow you to form any precise details.

Foam board

Foam card is made from three layers of material. The outer surfaces are good quality white cardboard and the inside is a thin layer of foam.

Foam card is light and can be glued to make simple models of buildings and rooms

Cardboard

Cardboard is probably the most widely used material for modelling. It can be made to look realistic by the addition of surface papers. Brick and tile patterns can be printed off from the computer and added to make a model of a house look realistic.

A model of a house using brick and tile patterns printed off from a computer

Thin plastic

Plastics, such as acrylic and polystyrene, can be used to make representational models. Acrylic can be heat-formed or used as a flat sheet. In the picture on the right, a scale model of a shop window design has been made from acrylic.

Using clay

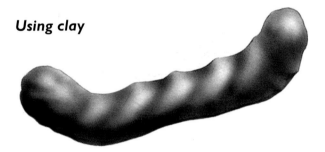

Squeezing clay in your hand can give you an idea about the best ergonomic shape for a handle.

Clay is useful to graphic designers. It is easy to use and bits can be easily added or taken away. It takes skill to produce detailed models but they are useful for testing concepts such as ergonomics.

Clay is also useful for making moulds for vacuum forming. Clay modelling is simple and quick and allows textures to be added.

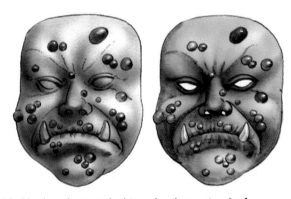

Marbles have been pushed into the clay to give the face a bumpy texture

Finishing off models

The most effective models look realistic. A wide range of different effects can be achieved with a little thought and imagination.

Finishes on plastic

Stained glass paint

It is often quite difficult to give the impression of a printed effect on plastic. However, designs can be hand-painted onto acrylic using special glass paints. These paints are water soluble and give a realistic finish to the work.

Fashion models hand-painted with stained glass paint

Spirit markers

Graphic marker binds to the surface of shiny plastic and does not scrape off. It can be used as an alternative to spray paint for colouring plastic sheet.

A model of a snowboard coloured using a graphic marker

To do

Find a piece of MDF board or acrylic sheet and glue as many flat texture objects to it as you can. When they have been glued, spray over the top of them with paint. This will produce an interesting texture board that will give you ideas about possible new modelling techniques.

Case study in design part I

This case study follows the real life design and making of a merchandizing pack. It is an example of how a large graphic products project can be carried out. Each section of the design process is highlighted.

Looking at promotion

The starting point for this project was to look at the area of promotion in order to identify a need or a good idea for a project.

Brainstorm of promotion

Brief

From the brainstorm the following brief was developed:

'Design and make a range of graphic products that will promote a new music shop.'

Learning from other products

Similar existing products were analysed to try and find out **key features** of successful designs. The use of colour, layout and typography were just some of the areas looked at.

Specification

A specification was then written to meet the design brief.

Specification

Time scale: The project needs to be completed in 14 weeks

Function: The main function of the pack is to promote the new music shop

Target market: Ages 14 – 25

Aesthetics: The designs must clearly relate to the music by using related images

Materials: The materials need to be light, waterproof, and easy to print onto

Ergonomics: The size of the products must be appropriate for the target market and the typography and layout should be easy to read

Cost: The cost should be relatively low because the promotion will only last for a short time

Research

Basic research was then carried out which showed the following results:

- The range of products should include a point of sale display, poster and credit card and gift voucher
- The main target market is 14–25
- Standard size paper and card – A4, A5 and A8 – should be used
- Four-colour printing should be used.

Design ideas

A range of initial design ideas was sketched and annotated.

I am looking at the idea of having for the logo, just the 5, and turning it into a sort of trademark or symbol of the company, like the big M for the McDonalds logo. When people see it they recognise it straight away, there's no need for writing.

This design is not appropriate for the logo as it is difficult to read and looks too old.

This design is better but from a distance it may look like an '5' which would not do.

This design could also be difficult to read from a distance as it is thin in places.

This design is very difficult to read as it could be mistaken for a 'b'.

This design is too thin so it wouldn't stand out from a distance.

This design is good because it is bold and clear

Initial design ideas for a logo

Development

During the development stage the use of ICT was important so that realistic graphics could be produced. Logo ideas were designed on the computer and could be easily modified. At this stage graphic models were produced, and these helped to evaluate the ideas against the intentions in the specification.

Once a successful logo was designed, it was time to start thinking about the different products that it could be used on. The credit card is a good example of this.

The design to the right is blue to right vertically. It looks good and the writing is legable but I want more of an emphasise on the '5'.

The design to the left is just right. I have moved the centre of the radial colouring behind the 5 which makes it stand out more.

To the right is the design it will be using and as you can see it works well with the blue and white radial background.

Developing a logo

When developing the designs it is important that all the standard graphical features of products are included. Bar codes, holograms, and existing logos may all be included to give the product a true-to-life look.

In order to achieve the appearance of shiny plastic, the designs for the credit card were printed onto photo quality paper. By making a three-tier sandwich with credit card designs on the outside and card in between, a realistic model can be made.

Development sketch of a credit card

Case Study in design part 2

Final design

The final design included a range of different products.

Some final designs

Flow chart for making a product

A flow chart was drawn up to show the stages in making the point of sale display unit.

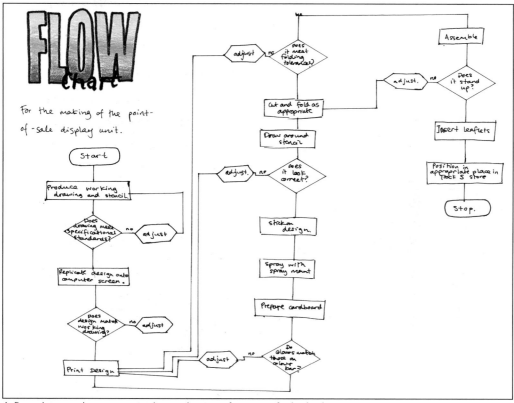

A flow chart to show stages in the production of a point of sale display

Presenting the products

Two-dimensional graphic products need to be presented in a display to show a client. Display albums are usually made from good quality coloured mounting card, which is joined with PVC insulation tape.

PVC insulation tape is used for the joins because it is very flexible. This is important because the album will be opened and closed many times.

Window mounting

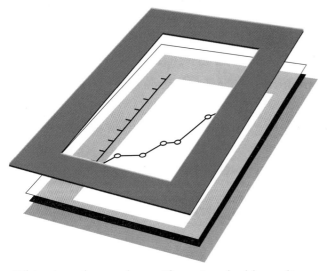

This gives the product a 'frame' and adds quality to the presentation.

With this technique a window is cut into the front piece of card and the product is glued onto the back.

The completed display album

Evaluation

The project was successful in meeting the needs of the specification. The use of the logo '5' on all the different products helps customers to relate them back to the company. The background design helps to create interest in the product and gives a sense of quality. The dark blue also helps the ergonomics by providing a contrast for the lettering which makes the products efficient to read. They certainly stand out.

I chose to use gold for some of the lettering. Gold gives the impression of best quality and this will make customers believe that the products are high quality.

The surface designs worked well. Using the scanner and photo editing software meant that I could produce a very realistic design. The photo paper gives a shiny finish. This is very important because all the leaflets that I looked at during my research had a glossy finish. I found out that this is produced by spraying a lacquer onto the paper when it is commercially printed. By using photo paper my designs look very true to life.

To do

The point of sale (P.O.S.) display stand that is used in this project has a special folding mechanism. Design a P.O.S. of your own that will allow the printer to print all the designs on one side, yet folds up so that all the text and images are the correct way up when it has been assembled.

Glossary

acrylic a brittle plastic commonly known as Perspex

adhesive a bonding agent used to join two materials

advertizing a means of promoting a product

aesthetics how various graphic elements combine to make a thing pleasing to the eye

alignment positioning of text on a page. Usually the text is aligned next to the margin (right or left) although it can be aligned to the centre line

analyse to study closely and ask questions like who?, what?, where?, when?, why? and how?

anthropometrics the study of measurements of human beings and their movements

batch production where a number of items are made at the same time

brainstorm a way of generating lots of ideas

brief a short statement of a problem or need

CAD computer-aided design

CAM computer-aided manufacture

clip art an electronic library of pictures

complementary colours colours opposite each other on a colour wheel and which go well together

consumer test a test that uses consumers to sample new products and give their opinions and preferences

continuous production when products are made one after the other

corporate identity the 'whole' graphic image of a company

criteria requirements of a product

cyberspace the name given to the Internet

database a collection of information stored on a computer program

design process the activity of solving problems through the development of ideas to produce a solution

development the process of taking an idea and improving/modifying it to achieve the best possible solution

digital camera a device which takes pictures and stores them directly on a computer disc

economies of scale the system which demonstrates that the cost of a single unit reduces as more are produced

elevation another name for the front or end 'view' on an orthographic drawing

e-mail (electronic mail) a means of sending information from one computer to another through a telephone line

ergonomics how products and places are designed to be efficient for humans to use

evaluation judgements made about ideas and products against the original specification

feint line a very lightly drawn line (often known as 'ghost line')

flow chart symbols used to graphically present a process

function what a product or process is expected to do

grid device used by graphic designers to help lay out a page

harmonizing colours colours that are neighbours on the colour wheel and go well together

horizon line the line of sight on a perspective drawing

hue the actual colour

isometric projection a method of three-dimensional drawing that uses lines drawn at 30°degrees

letterpress a simple form of printing

lithography a form of printing

logo (sometimes called 'logotype') a device used to help people associate a product with an organization

marketing the selling of a product or service to a consumer

mass production the production in large numbers of a product